Praise for Transcen[

"Maria's raw, authentic and relatable to so many. She shines light on the lessons and purpose that can be found once we move from resistance to acceptance. *Transcending Infertility* is a 'girlfriend's guide' to living with and learning from infertility. Her humor and vulnerability help empower the reader to move out of desperation and into peace on whatever their path may be."
– A'ndrea Reiter, Holistic Fertility Expert and author of *How to Get Pregnant Even When You've Tried Everything: A Mind Body Guide to Fertility*

"Beautifully weaving her professional expertise with her personal experiences, *Transcending Infertility* is a must-read for anyone who is experiencing the overwhelm of fertility challenges. A powerful book that empowers patients facing infertility to reclaim joy and hope."
– Parijat Deshpande, Bestselling author of *Pregnancy Brain*

"I absolutely loved this book. As someone who works with women struggling with infertility, I found myself highlighting things I wanted to share with my clients. And as a fellow human being, I found myself crying at parts of this book. It's powerfully moving and inspiring. I'd recommend it not only to women who are struggling with infertility, but anyone in their lives who wants to have a better understanding of what those women are going through. This book is a beautiful journey filled with hope, healing, and inspiration."
– Rachel Cook, HypnoFertility® practitioner

"Dr. Maria's words spoke to my soul and have helped me begin the process of healing my broken spirit. I am inspired and firmly believe that I can find meaning in my struggles and become a better person because of them. As both a mental health professional and a woman who has truly transcended infertility, Dr. Maria lends a unique perspective to the issue. She has bravely chosen to reveal a deeply personal side of herself for the benefit of her readers. This book is incredibly relatable, and I have no doubt that any woman struggling with infertility would find something that resonates with them. I have read many books about infertility, and this one is truly transformative. Give yourself the gift of self-care and read this book!"
– Jessica Wardell

"Your story will resonate with many women and men. So many of us seek perfection in ourselves and those around us. It is truly wonderful when you can start to see the beauty in the imperfect. Infertility is a subject surrounded in shame and secrecy. It is refreshing to hear someone in the profession tell their journey, openly and honestly. The keys you discuss can benefit all people, infertility or not. We all seek the same thing: unconditional love…for ourselves and others."
– Crystal O'Doherty

"I highly recommend this book to anyone who is experiencing or has experienced infertility. First, I must say that as a male who has walked the road of infertility alongside my wife every step of the way, it is critically important that BOTH partners in a relationship seek out support when going through infertility. For those of you at the beginning of the journey, marshal those support resources like *Transcending Infertility* now rather than later. Expect challenges, expect dark times, but know that the tools that Dr. Maria lays out will help you not only survive but thrive no matter how your infertility journey plays out. For those of you who are on the other side of infertility (though it never truly leaves you), the exercises and guided meditations that Dr. Maria provides in great detail will help you to understand how you've grown as a person, a partner, and a parent because of that difficult road. By weaving her own story in all its messiness and vulnerability, Dr. Maria teaches a set of clear keys, accompanied by concrete action steps and guided meditations that give you a clear course to navigate the challenge of infertility. If you read this book, follow the action steps, and use the guided meditations, you'll come out the other side recognizing that you are more powerful than you ever thought."
– Keegan Prue

"This is not one of those academically written self-help books. A raw and honest read, Dr. Maria Rothenburger writes *Transcending Infertility* from the space of having lived and breathed every real and imaginable fear and heartache from trying to conceive. The book teaches you to rise above the ashes of infertility to view life in a more meaningful and soulful way. It shows you how to use infertility as a tool for growth and personal development along the path to fulfilling your dream of being a parent, and from her own happy ending, it shows you that there is a silver lining to every dark cloud."
– Nadine Fahmy

Transcending Infertility

9 Keys for Improving Fertility, Creating Miracles, and Being a Better Human

Maria T. Rothenburger, PhD

Miracles Happen Fertility Center

Copyright ©2020 by Maria T. Rothenburger, PhD

All rights reserved. No part of this book may be reproduced, distributed, or transmitted in any form or by any means, including photocopying, recording, or other electronic or mechanical methods, without the prior written permission of the publisher, except in the case of brief quotations embodied in critical articles, reviews, and certain other noncommercial uses permitted by copyright law. This book comes from the author's heart and is here to support you in empowering yourself to create the life you desire. Please know, though, that it is not a replacement for therapy or medical advice. If you feel like you could use some extra support, please seek out a professional in your area.

Printed in the United States of America
ISBN: 978-1-7361498-0-5

Library of Congress Control Number: 2020922541

For T.

Thanks for hanging out in all of that fertility mud with me. You're pretty amazing. No, that doesn't mean I'll do the dishes more.

For O and B.

Miracles happen. You went and proved it. Thanks for choosing me, Weh-Weh and B-Boy. Mama loves you a billion times a gazillion.

Contents

Introduction: What IF 9

Chapter One: Hello, Infertility 19

Chapter Two: Quiet the Desperation 31

Chapter Three: Wearing Infertility Masks 53

Chapter Four: Stop Shoulding on Yourself 79

Chapter Five: Letting Go Is Not Giving Up 97

Chapter Six: Shrink IF 119

Chapter Seven: Trust Yourself 135

Chapter Eight: Be the Bamboo 157

Chapter Nine: What If Miracles Happen? 179

Chapter Ten: Dear Infertility 199

Conclusion: The Beginning 213

Acknowledgments 219

About the Author 221

Introduction

What IF

What If

These are two of the most powerful words in the universe. At once they can exude a sense of wonder for the potential of awesomeness, and they can crush the spirit with worries of impending doom. They are the diving board from which we jump into the pool of possibility.

"What if [insert good thing] happens?"

"What if [insert bad thing] happens?"

Coincidentally, IF are also the initials commonly used in the reproductive world when referring to infertility. It perfectly represents the waiting-to-exhale feeling my husband and I experienced during our six and a half years of trying to make a baby. If you too are among the growing population suffering from infertility, the following worrisome questions probably ring a bell. In fact, they likely hound you daily.

- What if I'm never a mom?
- What if this cycle doesn't work?
- What if I miscarry (again)?
- What if I get another baby shower invite?
- What if people pity me?

- What if I have to deal with one more frigging social media pregnancy announcement or one more April Fool's fake pregnancy announcement? I swear I will travel wherever is necessary to wring the necks of those idiots!

The What-If Syndrome is overwhelmingly powerful in the midst of infertility. And for the most part, the syndrome leans toward negative things happening rather than the possibility of something positive. You know exactly what I mean. You know the darkness. You know the loss. You know the heartbreak and despair. You know the intense longing, jealousy, confusion, ups and downs, disappointments, fear of the unknown, body judgment, and random snotty crying spells for no apparent reason (even though there's plenty of reason). If you are still flailing about in that darkness, this book is for you. And I'm giving you a virtual hug right this very moment.

If you are on the other side of the infertility trenches, you remember the darkness well. You will get plenty of information from this book you wish you would've had, and you can start using it now. Regardless of where you are in your journey, I encourage you to take this newfound knowledge and pay it forward, my friend. Someone else could use a little transcendence, don'tcha think?

Why Read This Book?

There are three major reasons for you to read this book:

1. I get you. Professionally and from personal experience, I know infertility well.
2. You will promote optimal fertility. (More on the science behind that is in your future.)
3. You will begin to live a life of joy and meaning rather than dealing with What-If Syndrome. If you put the principles in this book into practice, you will begin to see the miraculous in all things, and you will be a better version of yourself than you thought imaginable.

Let's get into more detail, shall we?

Reason Number 1: I Get You

I've wanted to be a psychotherapist since fifth grade. It's what I love to do, and through years of hard work and analyzing my husband—who was thrilled to contribute to the cause, of course—I did it. I hung my shingle. Then infertility showed up, and I felt like a psycho therapist. (Get it? Buh-DUM-dum-pshhhhhh. Thank you, thankyouverymuch. I'll be here all week.)

Anyway, just like in fifth grade (with a wee bit more training), I get to help people manage their emotional wellness. Ha! That's what my job description says. What I actually help people do is to not go bat-shit crazy in any given moment and perhaps take home a useful nugget or two for implementing when away from my office. Life is stressful! Throw infertility into the mix, and you've got yourself a ticket to What-the-Hell-Just-Happened-Ville.

So, here's a question for you: What happens when the therapist is the one trying not to go crazy? Like when she's trying to make a baby, and it's not working, and she's a child-and-family therapist and gets to see kids all day as well as their parents who sometimes mistreat them or devalue them or cannot understand the jewel they have in just being able to have a child in the first place? Oh irony, how I detest thee.

The point is, here I am, a therapist, and I still lost my mind through infertility.

There's this idea that therapists are supposed to know what to do to help themselves. I was supposed to have known how to handle the dark moments, the lack of support, and the shock of a medical diagnosis I couldn't understand and over which I had no control. I see this all day long from people who aren't even therapists. It doesn't matter who you are; it's completely okay if you've felt you've gone a bit off the deep end. I don't care if you're a former Buddhist monk; infertility will derail you.

Being a therapist, though, I decided that my best course of action was to go to therapy. (Surprise!) But guess what. It took me three tries before I found a therapist who didn't say things like, "Wow, I just look at my wife and she gets pregnant." Or "Have you tried relaxing?" Or my favorite, "Have you considered adoption?" Because, obviously, the path to pregnancy is adoption. (Insert sarcastic eye roll here.)

After finding a great therapist, I realized that the resources to heal from this tragedy were in me the whole time. Slowly—achingly slowly—I began to find my stride again. Not only did I find my stride, I was gliding. As my depression lifted, colors looked brighter, I found joy in the most mundane things, and I treated every interaction and experience with reverence. In short, everything was a miracle. Even more importantly, everything was a miracle before I became a mom. In fact, I had no idea what my next steps were. This is not a story of being better after finally achieving parenthood. This is a story of crawling through the muck and debris of infertility and coming out sparkly clean on the other side, showing off my scars even before I had my babies in my arms.

> This is not a story of being better after finally achieving parenthood. This is a story of crawling through the muck and debris of infertility and coming out sparkly clean on the other side, showing off my scars even before I had my babies in my arms.

That process is outlined in this book. Because of this book, you don't have to go through the trials and errors I did in order to find things that worked. No "achingly slowly" for you! Well, at least not slowly. There will likely be heartache, and I promise you, that's where the good stuff is. The bottom line is, I know infertility from a fellow "infertile's" experience as well as from a clinician's expertise. I know the bewilderment, sadness, worry, anger, sleepless nights, and relationship troubles. I also know the strategies that work to find peace again.

Reason 2: You Will Promote Optimal Fertility

Whoa. That's a friggin' giant claim, I know. To be entirely clear: This is not a book about how to get pregnant. I respect you enough to know that you should have an honorary Reproductive Medicine degree for everything you know about getting pregnant. However, I would be remiss if I didn't highlight the abundance of research on epigenetics and how our beliefs change our biology. You might not realize how much control you have over your body and its workings. This is more than nutrition and whether or not you should exercise during treatments, though those are important, too. The lessons in this book are about not thwarting all your amazing efforts by perpetually living in fear of the future or lamenting the past. Think about it. If you're constantly in a state of stress, your body receives the requisite signals and puts you in fight or flight. This is a no-go for fertility. You'll learn more about this throughout the book, including what happens to fertility when you're in a state of stress, as well as how to manage stress in a balanced way. Let's face it, we'll all experience stress for the rest of our lives, but you'll learn how to handle it effectively and reduce its negative impact on your body.

Probably the most exciting part of this book for me to share is the notion that movement toward optimal fertility doesn't stop at the level of the body. Everything we think, have emotions about, and resonate to is drawn to us. You've likely heard of the Law of Attraction and other such quantum realities. I'll touch on parts of these and offer insights into how you have more control over your body, mind, spirit, and destiny than you may have ever considered. Most importantly for your world right now, you'll be given specific strategies to try immediately in order to move toward optimal fertility.

Reason 3: You'll Begin to Live a Life of Joy and Meaning Rather Than Dealing with What-If Syndrome

I'm an eternal optimist. But if I'm totally honest, infertility stole my rose-colored glasses for a spell. This book is raw. Sometimes it's downright dark. I recall moments of utter despair when I believed I was doing this in complete solitude. I write the raw, dark moments so you understand you're normal, even though you feel like your mind is going to implode from the newest wave of irrationality. Perhaps more importantly, you'll see that you're not alone, even though it feels like nobody around you has the slightest idea how to help, or worse, they say things that tear your heart open when it has barely healed from the last blow. But most importantly, this book highlights how the dark moments can graciously accentuate the light, serving as jumping-off points for growth, healing, and heretofore unimagined peace. It wasn't until the middle of my journey to parenthood that I finally started noticing the light that was always there. I'll write that again: The light was always there.

You don't have to wait as long as I did. You don't have to wait at all. The lessons in this book are the gifts infertility gave me. Don't get me wrong; infertility blows. It's a gross understatement to say it broke my spirit. But it was also the impetus that changed my world in vast ways I may have only glossed over were it not for my newfound understanding. I've passed these lessons on to my clients, and now I'm honored to share them with you.

Notice I did not write that you'll emerge wholeheartedly positive and unerringly optimistic, making people wonder whether you were Pollyanna in a past life. Being positive all the time is not at all what I am writing about. In fact, as one of my favorite teachers, Deepak Chopra, says, "Even a positive mind is a turbulent mind." The keys within are about quieting the mind, noticing both the crap and the wonderful aspects of infertility without judgment and without needing them to change. The more you want things to be different from how they are, the more stress you'll create for yourself and the people around you.

Using the Fertility Keys, you'll learn to live from curious possibility. What the heck does that mean, you ask? I want you to imagine that a company has just given you a fantastic product to try out and see what you think. Let's imagine it's an amazing high-tech gadget. With curiosity, you start pushing buttons, moving it around, and observing the outcome. You approach this cool new toy with curiosity. "I wonder what would happen if I pushed this button?" That's what I mean by curious possibility. Get curious without judgment, without turmoil, and with the calm attitude of a service dog who gently places a firm paw on her charge's arm to alert of an oncoming seizure. Total awareness. Total focus. And total calm. Can you imagine if you had that level of peace while waiting to know if your next cycle produced a miracle? After putting these Fertility Keys into practice, you'll be able to do more than imagine it. You'll live it.

I know it can seem far-fetched to consider living a life of joy and meaning while experiencing infertility. Most people believe that those things come after resolving infertility. Let me clear up this myth: People can still very much suffer from the trauma of infertility even after they have their precious babies in their arms. Conversely, you can work through the trauma and reach emotional wellness even before resolving infertility.

If that didn't blow your mind, this will: In this book, I'm proposing one step further. You need not stop at healing from infertility trauma. I'm proposing that you can be a better human because of infertility. I'm proposing that you can feel a deep sense of gratitude and even (gasp!) honor the infertility experience as one that was ultimately beneficial. I'm talking about a deep sense of knowing and profound meaning driven from having experienced the soul-crushing weight of the infertility beast. I'm talking about being the part of you on a daily basis that feels safe, that knows you can handle whatever comes your way, that feels loved and loving, and that knows why you experienced the darkness. What I wish for you is to be able to examine your experience of infertility and say, "I get it now. It sucked. And I get it now. Thank you."

How to Use This Book

If you read even one chapter from this book, my hope is that you're able to walk away with a couple of nuggets. Sometimes just reading another's story helps alleviate the pain of isolation. Sometimes reading someone's insight helps you see your own story in a different light. If that's enough for you, you've done well. That said, each chapter contains suggestions for cultivating the healing that I and many of my clients experienced during each point I write about. You're encouraged to engage in each small exercise in any way you wish. Even thinking about it helps the growth process. However, you are absolutely free to read this book like a novel. After all, at the core, this is a story of overcoming tragedy and opening up to immense joy.

In my work with clients, I've come to realize that what I offer as Fertility Coaching is actually Fertile Life Coaching. That is, everything I talk about can be used throughout life. After all, the essence of fertility is creation, right? Everything you learn in these pages goes beyond your baby-making journey and right into creating miracles throughout your life. As you read, you'll move toward optimal fertility and optimal livelihood. My goal for you is that after you've read this book and put the skills into action, you'll thrive as a human. This is true no matter how you choose to continue your fertility journey. In addition, thriving as a human may happen **because** of your fertility journey. That is what it means to truly transcend adversity.

> What I offer as Fertility Coaching is actually Fertile Life Coaching. That is, everything I talk about can be used throughout life. As you read, you'll move toward optimal fertility and optimal livelihood.

Each chapter is broken down into several sections:

- **The Why** – Here I talk about why the chapter is important for you in your fertility journey.
- **Story** – This section is my personal story (gulp), mistakes and all. In it, you'll find the reasons why these lessons became incredibly important for my growth and why I chose to teach others.
- **Action Steps** – This section is exactly what the name implies: It's where you take action. I note several practical exercises you can use in your own life to gain the skill necessary to learn the Fertility Key. I suggest taking ten days per key to create your own ninety-day program.

Two fundamental parts of this program are making use of a journal and incorporating meditation into your daily life. Each chapter has a meditation you can begin working with. You can access recordings to all the meditations at www.drmariarothenburger.com/transcendingmeditations. I encourage you to use your journal and do the meditations, but don't worry—I won't send the Journal and Meditation Police to force you. However, if you don't utilize these tools, you'll greatly reduce your ability to still your mind and track your progress.

That said, remember that nothing in this book is about perfection. Actually, I adhere to a strict policy of screwing up. Like, a lot. Because that is the only way to get better. All new behaviors come from starting small, not by being perfect.

Important Note

The following content is not meant to replace professional help. If you are seriously struggling with the emotional effects of infertility, I highly recommend that you find a therapist, coach, counselor, doctor, energy worker, shaman, or other helping professional adept in improving emotional wellness while dealing with this life-changing health condition.

Finally, the lessons I write here are my own. But after working with countless women and men on their journey to parenthood, I know that the potential for growth and peace is in all of us. I know that some people—after careful consideration of life through infertility—choose to recognize the gifts, too. What if you're one of them?

Here's What's Coming Up

- **Chapter 1: Hello, Infertility** – This is where the story begins. Infertility, trauma, my control-freak self, and the unhelpful things well-meaning people tried to settle my crazed wanna-be-mom self.
- **Chapter 2: Quiet the Desperation** – You and desperation have gotten to know each other quite well, haven't you? Unfortunately, desperation is toxic for your fertility, and it's time to break up. This chapter is all about how to do so.
- **Chapter 3: Wearing Infertility Masks** – If you've been dealing with infertility, you likely know how to fake that all is well. This is what I call "wearing your infertility mask." It's exhausting—and just plain annoying—to pretend you're someone you're not. On the other hand, masks are useful when you need to protect yourself. This chapter is about donning your mask wisely.
- **Chapter 4: Stop Shoulding on Yourself** – Do you ever beat yourself up? Yeah, I'm probably reading your mind right now. This chapter helps you identify and begin changing your "coulda-shoulda-woulda" language toward yourself (and others).
- **Chapter 5: Letting Go Is Not Giving Up** – This is a tough one. Letting go of your dream seems like total failure, doesn't it? Yet it's not. This chapter explains how letting go is essential for your fertility

and is the complete opposite of giving up on your dream of parenthood.

- **Chapter 6: Shrink IF** — You've made infertility your whole world. That sucks. And truthfully, you've lost yourself in the process. Who are you anyway? Get yourself back by putting infertility back in its rightful place: important but not everything.

- **Chapter 7: Trust Yourself** — You know that thing where we seek to follow social norms (like date someone, get married, buy a house with a picket fence, and have 2.5 children)? What if you don't have to do that? What if you could attend to your inner guidance and instantly know your best move toward parenthood? This chapter helps you access your inner guidance system and understand your true power.

- **Chapter 8: Be the Bamboo** — Even with the best-laid plans, shit happens. It's incredibly important to know how to move through hard times when they hit us. Rather than getting stuck, you're capable of letting hard times pass through you while you wait—bending but not breaking, like a bamboo tree in strong wind.

- **Chapter 9: What If Miracles Happen?** — In this chapter, I ask you to get fully into the headspace of wondering what would happen if positive things were always on their way to you. It's a profound shift in how you experience life by merely thinking and engaging with your world differently. You don't want to miss the story in this chapter or the practical skills to get your miracles on!

- **Chapter 10: Dear Infertility** — "Dear" and "infertility" don't belong in the same sentence, right? Or do they? In this final lesson, I present to you my letter to infertility. Raw and honest, it is truly a lesson that brings home the point "be a better human."

Before you get started on these lessons, please take out your journal and write this down: "I don't know where this journey will take me, but I am willing to go. I am open to this experience, and I am worthy of positive change, just because I'm showing up."

Now let's get this party started.

Chapter One

Hello, Infertility

All the world is full of suffering. It is also full of overcoming.
— Hellen Keller

Control. Freak.

When I was sixteen, some friends and I had a conversation about all our troubles. You know how teens are. This one had way too much homework, that one had boy issues, and another hated her parents. I, on the other hand, gleefully and obnoxiously stated, "My only problem is that I have no problems."

What a liar.

Like any angsty teen, I was painfully hyperaware of how others saw me. You know that zit on my nose? Yeah, everybody saw it, and they were talking about how gross it was behind my back. Obviously, I was the center of the universe, so they had to talk about me. Right? I had an extremely strong aversion to vulnerability. Nobody could possibly know of the horrors in my mind. I wouldn't let them. They didn't know I wasn't smart enough, pretty enough, thin enough, or just plain good enough because I had successfully fooled them all. Damn, I was good.

The mask was a constant in my life, and I wore it well. "Oh, Maria? She's doing great! She always does great!" I had portrayed an image of myself I wanted everyone to see, but of course, she wasn't the real me. On the outside, I was the picture of perfection. I got decent grades, had a long-term boyfriend, was the first choir girl to win homecoming queen in my high school (even though I tied with a cheerleader), never did drugs, never drank alcohol, and surely never went to parties where a responsible adult wasn't present at all times.

Of course, Ms. Chaos had taken up residence inside me a long time prior. It probably had something to do with divorced parents, absentee dad, mean stepdad, and being constantly teased in grade school for being the fat, nerdy kid who was teacher's pet. I learned that if I attempted to control my outside world, everything would feel manageable inside. Before I had it "right," my tumultuous adolescent self developed an eating disorder, but nobody really liked that too much. Uh-oh! I had to be socially acceptable! Okay, scratch the eating disorder. Eventually, I started to portray that aforementioned picture-perfect life. People liked that. They gave me thumbs up, head nods, and smiles. They said they were proud of me.

So, let me get this straight. All I have to do to be "good enough" is follow a series of steps to accomplish more goals? I can totally do that! I mean, the steps are already laid out, right? And they work every time. I need only walk the proverbial yellow brick road, and Oz shall reward me with being good enough every single time. Friggin' piece of cake.

Not So Fast, Dorothy

I was plugging along just fine in my accomplish-more-and-you'll-be-awesome life. I had moved from the west to the east coast to be with the love of my life. We were married, owned a cute starter home, and had a yellow lab. If my life were a recipe, the directions would read, "Just Add Picket Fence." I was on the verge of a master's degree in counseling, and I was looking forward to ditching the mortgage industry for my real career as a psychotherapist. I'd figured out pretty early on that people gravitated toward me for life advice. In fact, it's one of the reasons I felt that people really believed I had my shit together. I was perfecting this control thing.

Don't get me wrong; there were a few slip-ups along the way. Like that time I blew up the engine in my '79 Honda Accord hatchback, or the time I figured it was totally okay to bake bread in a bread maker without removing the cardboard packaging first. Then there was the time I decided to—gasp!—engage in premarital sex. (Sorry, Mom.) But I have to say, I always, always used birth control. There was no way a baby was going to mar this perfect life. (Hello, irony.)

The day we decided to build our family was momentous. Even though we didn't have a white picket fence, we felt the timing was perfect, so I promptly stopped taking birth control. I thought, "Everyone has told me since seventh grade that if you don't use birth control, you'll get pregnant. So as soon as I stop, I'll get pregnant. Yay!" Well, guess what. I did!

My husband and I were sitting on our back patio on a hot August afternoon after the digital home-pregnancy test showed "Pregnant." We were ecstatic of course, and I was already rubbing my barely pregnant belly. My husband, T, held his muscle-laden arms high and exclaimed in his thick New Jersey, "Yeah, I knew it! I bet there's three o' dem in there!" My whole life I had dreamed of a baby with dimples because they run in my family. And oh! Wouldn't it be amazing if he was a lefty like both T and me? Obviously it's going to be a boy because we want a boy first. Three years after that we'll have our girl. T dreamed of coaching little league, and I dreamed of breast-feeding while angels sang. Bliss!

Because I was blessed with obsessive tendencies, I took another pregnancy test the next day. This time the display read "Negative." Confused, I took five more tests all with the same mocking display. What the…? Two weeks later I still hadn't gotten my period, so I made an appointment for the gynecologist, who told me I probably had a "chemical pregnancy." What does that even mean? I was pregnant, and now I'm not? I don't get it. He said this happens all the time, and I'd be fine. Just keep trying, he said.

Enter Infertility

The following months began the increasingly frantic attempts to get pregnant again. I thought, "This will be easy. The doc said it would, and he's the doc, right? So obviously I'll be pregnant next month."

I said that every cycle for the next six months. I dutifully checked my fertility signs and learned way more about my body than I thought most people know. I knew when my cervix was open, my body was ready for sperm by show of egg-white cervical mucus, and I had gauged pretty accurately my "fertile window" (the several days before ovulation). I had followed all the steps, so clearly I would meet the end goal.

Nope.

It was here that I felt a wee bit of a crack in my psyche. I didn't understand this new thing where I followed all the rules and I still didn't achieve what I had set out to achieve. What the hell was happening?

Control freaks must have a next thing to do; that's how we roll. Therefore, I made my plans for next steps. Next on the list: Visit another doctor. This one looked at my perfectly notated charts and interpreted them as I was ovulating too late. "I'll put you on a little Clomid; you'll be fine. You'll be pregnant in six months." Instead, I reached the twelve-month mark of trying to conceive and was officially diagnosed with infertility.

Heart. Break.

Losing It

My brother once joked with me that I did everything right. I graduated high school, went to college, got a good job, got married, all in that order. Sure, I moved in with my boyfriend before we were even engaged, but my mom liked him, so it was all good. Both of my brothers, on the other hand, were fathers at eighteen, and my younger sister was the proverbial black sheep, always off doing her own thing. I was "the good one." I was the one who was always on the right path. So it didn't make sense, my brother said, that I'd be the one to have trouble having kids. It was as if one earns the right to bear children by merit alone. It's one of the things that perplexes many people struggling with infertility: If crack addicts and others who abuse their bodies and don't have their life together can get pregnant easily, why do I have such trouble? It didn't make sense.

As I soon learned, though, "sense" had nothing to do with it. Even with science and treatment on my side, I was not a mom, and that is why I was losing it. I was losing my cool, losing my calm, and losing my ability to keep on keeping on. The following journal entry captures this perfectly:

> I cannot possibly describe the anguish I felt just now in writing the date. It's been four more ridiculously expensive, hopeful, depressing, anxious, angry, doubtful, heartbroken months since my failed IUI. I just got my period this evening, as T and I were packing for our weekend trip to VA to meet up with my parents. I ignored the familiar lower back sensations again all day and even imagined what it would be like to get a positive on a pregnancy test. I felt such joy!
>
> And now I feel incredible sorrow. I am searching (begging even) for the light at the end of the tunnel. Where the fuck is it, God?! Please!! I can't take this much longer!! Give me some help—some direction!! I don't know what the fuck else to do besides what I've been doing! The frustration is incredible—how does one carry on in this state? It's impossible. I want serenity—God please help me!! I'm going to crack.

And I did crack. Wide open.

What Infertility Is Like

Conceiving is so natural, right? It should be easy. It's what our miraculous bodies are made to do. We're scared to death in middle school when we take that embarrassing co-ed sex-education class and are told in no uncertain terms: "Protection, protection, protection, or you *will* get pregnant or get someone else pregnant." It was practically guaranteed. So when conception does not come easily, we're stunned. And shamed. Yet we hide our shame by acting as if all is normal in the land of milk and honey, even though our light diminishes more and more with each passing month.

We walk by families and yearn for the joy on their faces, or even to be that frazzled mother who gives her kid a popsicle just to shut him up. We plead to the Universe for an experience like that. Watching cute, pregnant women waddle by, we think, "I'd love to have those water-ballooned ankles. I know they're probably not comfortable, but I'd do anything to have the promise of what she has." Every waking moment becomes an obsession about becoming a parent. And everywhere we look, we're reminded of what we don't have. Suddenly, baby ads, baby products, baby stores, nursery rhymes, pregnant women, and all things related to that which we cannot have are in our face like a one-two punch from Mr. Balboa himself.

If you're having trouble relaying to others what infertility is like, you're not alone. Consider explaining it to them through an imaginary journey that nearly everyone can relate to: Imagine you've gotten accepted into your university of choice. You arrive brimming with possibility. The first semester is filled with prerequisite classes, some of which you're not that interested in, but you take them anyway because that's just part of the process. Over the next few semesters, you know what to do because you check in regularly with your advisor. You have a clear plan for how to graduate. But it's hard. Whew! You didn't know it would be so hard. By your final year, you've pulled at least a hundred all-nighters prepping for exams and creating projects. You've kept your GPA up because you had a plan and knew exactly what to do.

You finally reach the end of your final year and are about to graduate. Everyone is there to witness this amazing event. Commencement is here! You even have people streaming the event live on the internet, since they couldn't be there. This is a crowning achievement! You are graduating summa cum laude, and your family is so proud. They expected this of you, of course. After all, you've always had your plan laid out and your head in the game, and you followed the steps to a T.

So, you wait in line for your name to be called. You see some of your classmates crossing the stage, adorned with their stately robes and huge smiles. When the dean of their department hands them their diploma with a graceful sweep, they stop for a quick photo, then they're off the stage and headed to their just-graduated-from-college life. You're imagining what that will be like for you. And you're getting goosebumps thinking about how all the effort of college has been worth it just to reach this moment.

Suddenly, your name is called. You're jolted back to the moment, and you climb those stairs without a hitch. "No tripping for me! This is my day," you think. With twinkling eyes and wide grin, you practically float toward the dean, who turns toward you and says, "I'm sorry, but there's no diploma for you today. You're not graduating. There was an error, and you have to start from the beginning."

"Um, what??" you ask. "What happened? I did everything right! I followed the whole protocol without a hitch!"

"That's right, you did," the dean says. "We don't know what went wrong. But you still have to start over. So sorry."

You walk off the stage in a daze. People are looking at you like, "Hmm, I wonder what she did wrong." Your family is perplexed, and they start giving you all kinds of advice. You hear them, but you're not really listening. Once you're out of the bewilderment stage, you move on to the rest of the grief stages, eventually leading to starting the program over again. But upon graduation the second time, the dean says the same thing: "We don't know why it didn't work this time. Let's give it another go."

Over time, a dark shadow starts to form over you. You feel like you can't move forward with your life until you complete this step. You watch all your peers in their careers, and you can't even speak with them because you have nothing in common anymore. You can't plan for vacations or have any fun at all because a) you have to pay for college and b) you have to scrutinize every little detail of your academics and have to at least be near the university in case a professor offers you extra credit or something.

Everything around you reminds you that you haven't managed to graduate yet. You start to feel shame. Why isn't this happening for me? It works so easily for everyone else! I'm doing everything the professors and my advisors are telling me to do!

Years go by. Your friends have kids who are in school now. If you're one of the lucky ones, your family is sensitive, kind, understanding, and supportive. If you're not, you're rejected, judged, yelled at, shamed, and ultimately separated from a core unit you've known your whole life. In short, it's utter devastation. And it seems like nobody understands.

I hope this little story helps someone in your life have the smallest glimmer of what you're going through. At the very least, you deserve understanding.

Unhelpful Things

People who don't truly understand infertility tend to offer the most perplexing advice and placations. Of course, there are a few people who are intentionally harmful, due to their own stuff, but the vast majority want to be helpful. Here are a few of the statements I personally heard:

- "Are you sure you're—ya know—doing it right?"
- "Oh honey, just get drunk and have sex. Worked for us!"
- "Geez, I just look at my wife and she gets pregnant." (This one from therapist #2)
- "You need to just relax. Go on vacation!"
- "In God's time."
- "If it's meant to be, it's meant to be."
- "Well, at least you have each other."
- "Hey, at least you can **get** pregnant!" (After hearing of a miscarriage)
- "You know, so many kids out there need good homes. You should just adopt."
- "You're young! You have so much time left!"

Everyone out there struggling with conceiving has heard at least half of these. But wait, there's more! How about some crude jokes, like these?

- "Make sure you tell the doc to put the right sperm back in!"
- "Please, you can totally have one of my kids."
- "Hey! I'll rent you my uterus!"
- "Well, uh…I'd be happy to donate the sperm." [Wink, wink. Grabs crotch]
- "OMG, so if you think about it, technically the doctor is knocking you up!"

And then, there are the cruel and humiliating judgments:

- "Wow, well if you do IVF, don't ever tell the baby. It'll just traumatize him."
- "Wait, you're using someone else's eggs? Do you think you'll even love the baby the same?"
- "Wait, you're using someone else's sperm? Won't that make your husband feel like less of a man?"
- "What if the donor is like an axe murderer or something?"
- "You're not coming to my baby shower just because you can't have a baby? That's selfish and stupid!"

If you've heard even a fraction of the above statements, I'm sending you like a billion times a gazillion hugs through the ether. Nobody should have to feel such shame, embarrassment, and cruelty from anyone else. Ever. Infertility is a medical condition, not a choice. Infertility is a trauma, not a personality issue. Please stop reading now and go ask someone for a hug. And if there is nobody around, give yourself a hug.

Note: If you have made one of these statements to someone struggling to conceive, give yourself a hug, too. It's not your fault. I know that you mean well. The same is true for most people—they truly want to be helpful but simply don't have the proper tools or words that could offer potential healing and support. For example, asking your loved one what they need rather than assuming is a great start. Another wonderful skill is to refrain from trying to fix anything (usually starts with "Have you tried…?"). Because you've read this, you can do better next time. With knowledge comes change, and I honor your change and growth through reading this today.

Speaking of Trauma

Somewhere in the midst of weird and hurtful comments, somewhere among the monthly hope and desperate yearning for a baby, I came alive. The trauma of infertility had sucked me in, and I felt absolutely empty inside. As the pages of this book will illustrate for you, it's quite an understatement to say I wasn't a happy camper. But there was a point when a shift was created, even before I had my baby in my arms. I couldn't understand what had happened there; so, true to "control freak" nature, I began researching. I wanted to find out why I was so happy. Plenty of people who were on the "other side" of infertility still carried bitterness with them on the daily, constantly lamenting their plight as one who did not get to conceive in the privacy of their bedroom on the first try.

During my research, I came upon a concept called Posttraumatic Growth (PTG), which absolutely blew my mind. Make no mistake, infertility is a traumatic life event likened to the emotional difficulties of a cancer diagnosis. It is not for the faint of heart. However, according to the research on PTG, it's entirely possible to not only recover from trauma but to be better than you used to be because you had to go through such hardship. The questions floated around in my mind: Could this be what I was experiencing? Why was I so happy even though things hadn't worked in my favor yet? Shouldn't I have had a baby, then experience PTG? So many questions! I won't hold you in suspense for long. The answer is, yes, I was experiencing PTG. It doesn't matter that I didn't have a baby yet; PTG can happen any time.

> It's entirely possible to not only recover from trauma but to be better than you used to be because you had to go through such hardship.

Researchers have narrowed PTG down to five domains: Personal Strength, New Possibilities, Relating to Others, Appreciation of Life, and Spiritual Change. Imagine if all these areas of life were better for you? What would life look like? How would it be different?

Have you ever heard someone say, "I'm stronger than I thought I was"? Maybe it was even you! Have you ever stopped to consider other options for your life moving forward in a different way than you thought? It can be scary and exciting at the same time. This book is meant to help you make infertility useful, to help you see that there are myriad possibilities for your life right now outside of feeling stuck all the time.

What's Next?

The following pages explore nine Fertility Keys that I've found, personally and professionally, to yield the most change in one's psyche during infertility. I will not only explain these keys in detail, I'll show you how I developed them through my own experience either by (ahem) screwing up or by using them successfully.

Now, it's all fine and dandy to promote emotional and psychological growth while dealing with infertility, right? But guess what. You can also improve your biology through emotional and psychological growth! Several decades' worth of studies have shown that we're much more in control of our bodies than most people think we are. Your thoughts affect your biology. More on the science behind this later. For now, following this line of science and logic, if you're having constant negative thoughts about your struggles with conceiving, your cells will receive those messages and respond in kind.

Am I saying you're at fault for your infertility? Absolutely not! If you didn't have the information to make a wise choice, there's not a whole lot of responsibility you can claim. Take the above examples where people say hurtful things. Is it their fault their words are hurtful? No, they aren't aware that those statements are painful for you and are simply saying what's on their mind. These are statements, by the way, that are likely socially conditioned, this-is-just-what-you-say statements, like at a funeral when people ask, "How are you holding up?" It's unlikely to be a helpful question. It's merely socially conditioned. Not their fault. But, as the wonderful Maya Angelou said, "When you know better, you do better." Use this book to begin doing better. I truly hope that the material in these pages resonates with you and that you begin to practice these Fertility Keys in your own life.

Chapter Two

Quiet the Desperation

It is a characteristic of wisdom not to do desperate things.
— Henry David Thoreau

Picture this: A gazelle is grazing on some new shoots of grass in a wide-open meadow. Her entire herd is nearby, all lazily enjoying the morning sunshine and the sounds of nature all around. She slowly chews her food, intermittently looking up to scan her environment and enjoy every nuance of the experience. She's in the moment.

Suddenly, one of her comrades flicks its tail in a way that alerts her to a threat. As one, the entire herd begins to run away from the threat. Knowing she can no longer feed, the gazelle stops chewing the grass she had in her mouth. Her extremities are filled with blood after her brain sent out a whole host of signals saying, "Run! Lion!" Sure enough, a hunting lion and her crew are chasing after the gazelles, hoping for a successful kill to bring home to the rest of the pride.

The gazelle runs amidst a flurry of racing hearts, pumping lungs, cortisol, adrenaline, and fast-moving limbs. The chase lasts for quite a while, with the gazelle dodging every lion's attempt at snagging her and feeding her to the pride. Nonessential bodily functions have ceased to work. The grass she swallowed a few minutes before stays where it was, no longer moving through her stomach to be digested. She barely notices the knot of indigestion as she works through the current explosion of chemicals and signals to run for her life. Her reproductive organs—nonessential for living—have also shut down. Her body knows instinctively that she is in no place to attempt to procreate right now. She needs to survive.

The chase begins to wind down as the lions tire from their rapid burst of energy, no longer able to sustain the speed at which the gazelles glide across the landscape. The lions eventually come to a halt, realizing their hunt was not successful, and they turn around to head back to the pride.

The gazelle, having sensed a shift in the energy, looks around at her comrades. All their hearts continue to pump, their muscles full of adrenaline and the nourishing blood required to effectively utilize the muscles needed while running for one's life. Once they realize the lions have stopped their chase, however, the gazelles also slow down to a more casual pace. After a few minutes, they go back to grazing. Our little gazelle does not notice the ball in her stomach from the undigested food prior to the chase because digestion begins to pick up again. After a few more minutes, the gazelle is completely calm, as if the lions had never intruded upon her day. She's peaceful, slowly tasting her food, being in the moment with her comrades, occasionally looking up from her morning snack to scan her environment again. She looks like she has nary a care in the world.

What's the difference between the gazelle and us? If we were the gazelle, we would relive the moment when the lions crested the hill and the fear set in. We would replay it over and over in our minds, and our bodies would respond in kind. And when a trauma like infertility crests the hill of our life, we rarely resume our once-peaceful grazing. Instead, we live in a constant state of shock and fear.

The beauty and the curse of our gorgeous brain is that it doesn't know the difference between memories and thoughts based in the present. It also doesn't know whether our thoughts are future oriented. It still floods the bloodstream with chemicals that match the corresponding thoughts. Think about what this means for someone dealing with infertility. To receive a difficult medical diagnosis is hard enough. Yet here's what the brain does when a medical diagnosis feels traumatic: It. Remembers. Every. Single. Detail. Yeah, you know your favorite sweater you wore the day your Reproductive Endocrinologist (RE) said you should consider donor eggs? Your brain remembers that (and probably wants to throw the sweater out). Remember walking into the clinic for your follow-up appointment to your last failed cycle (lovingly referred to in the fertility community as the "what the fuck" appointment)? Your brain recalls every single thing from that moment. Driving into the parking lot, parking, walking into the clinic, pushing the elevator button, the smell of the hallway headed to your RE's office, the familiar door, the sounds of the clinic's hustle and bustle, the nurse's voice, the waiting-area chair's upholstery—everything. If you're anything like me and many others who have experienced this, you moved through that space as if in a dream, but your brain is not likely to forget all those details.

The struggle with having such an amazing memory system is that we also have a memory for the emotions residing alongside the images, sensations, sounds, and smells in our mind. That's what makes it difficult to move through trauma. So, if our lovely little gazelle friend were to live like us, she'd be having intense, horrifying, desperate emotions most of her day and perhaps even in her dreams. But the gazelle is different from us in that she knows that lions are life threatening, yet she's able to live in the now. And right now, there is no lion. By sharp contrast, we humans can feel like we're being chased by a lion when we're lathering up in the shower, brushing our teeth, and driving to work. If you're dealing with infertility, it can feel like the entire pride is stalking you each time you pass a baby store or anticipate a baby-shower invite when you get your mail.

Our bodies are meant to handle temporary gazelle-like stress, but they're not meant to sustain chronic stress. In fact, the science of epigenetics is showing that chronic stress triggers the expression of our individual unhealthy genes. Discussing this topic, developmental biologist Bruce Lipton says, "You can come with the most perfectly healthy set of genes possible, but if you live in a world of chronic fear and stress, you can generate every disease on this planet." Your genes are merely a blueprint for what is to be expressed in your outer world. It's your consciousness that controls what your genes do. This is completely backward from what we've been told for many years.

The fact is, you're a powerhouse in your own life and through your journey to parenthood. The more you realize how much control you have over what symptoms are expressed in your body, the freer you become. Can you imagine what you would change about your infertility if you put your thoughts to it?

> **The more you realize how much control you have over what symptoms are expressed in your body, the freer you become.**

There's a formal exercise on this under "Action Steps" in this chapter, but for now, I'd like you to put this book down, pause, and think of a simple non-fertility thing you'd like to change about your body's functioning. For example, I'd like for my nails to stop being so flaky. Super simple. Now, imagine that small thing in your body being different, being just the way you'd like it to be. We'll get into more detail about this later. For now, simply notice the difference between what it feels like to imagine the thing you don't like about your body compared to your body experiencing perfect health. For instance, I'm imagining perfectly strong, healthy, shiny, thick nails. I notice a sensation of calm, being at ease, even happiness. I even notice the tiniest tingling sensations at my fingertips. Compared to thoughts of the flakiness, these new thoughts feel so much lighter. What do you notice?

When you put your body through the impact of chronic fear, it will inevitably show the results. However, the flip side of this is that when you put your body through the impact of chronic love—when you quiet the desperation that is infertility—your body will inevitably show the requisite results. You may be asking, "Well that's all well and good, Maria, but how do you suggest I do this?" That's what this entire book is about! I should preface this and the following chapters with the notion that all the skills you'll learn are simple, yet they're not necessarily easy. What I suggest is that you give them some effort—absolutely without desperation. Get curious. Say to yourself, "I wonder what will happen when I do this." This is a thousand miles from, "Okay, I'm going to add this to the list, so I can check it off my how-to-be-more-fertile checklist!" The latter is desperation talking, and I encourage you to uninvite desperation from your life toward parenthood, which is exactly what I chose to do.

The following is the humble beginning of my journey to parenthood, which involved a crap ton of desperation. I'm not unlike you. I'm not infallible. Also, I love lists. I love creating them and giving myself the opportunity to check off all that I've accomplished. What can I say? It worked for me historically, and I knew it would work for making a baby, too. Ah, I sometimes miss the bliss of baby-making naïveté. This chapter is replete with my inordinate mistakes in holding on to desperation while trying to build our family. Knowing what I know now, I can look back and see how my body began to deteriorate from that state of chronic fear. For now, I shall take you back to the beginning.

Confessions of a Dr. Google Addict

When I was eleven, my sixth-grade class got a computer. I'm completely dating myself by noting how fantastic a deal this was, but what the heck. It. Was. Awesome! We were to learn basic programming in order to make a cool picture and present it to the class. I still remember the bright-colored clown I created. He even had a flower in his hat and a big red bow. I also recall the balloons I put in each corner and how I didn't have enough time to program one of the corners. It still bothers me.

It was many years later before I got my own computer, and by then, this nifty little thing called the world wide web had come to fruition. I didn't quite understand the internet, frankly. It was too fast, too spacious. I still very much preferred the familiar smell, feel, and sound of the card catalog at the library. And there's nothing quite like the weight of an encyclopedia in my arms to evoke the eager anticipation of exploration. My mouth is literally watering as I write. Such delight! And total nerdiness. I love it.

Alas, the digital age was upon us when infertility struck, and there wasn't an encyclopedia in the world that could satiate my incessant desire to know more. On the subject of infertility, I was a voracious and obsessive learner. In the free moments I'd usually spent playing with the dogs, walking, crocheting, cooking (or rather, trying to cook), talking with friends, or any other normally fun thing, I now spent hunched over a keyboard, fixated on whatever the internet had to tell me that day about making a baby. I could not—would not—stop. I was a Dr. Google addict.

After twelve months of trying unsuccessfully to make a baby, things began sucking. I had been on Clomid for six of those months, and I finally felt compelled to check out a reproductive endocrinologist's help rather than the OB/GYN who told me everything would be totally fine. I knew that everything was not fine, and I needed answers to why that was. It's amazing how different the world looks when one has the best-laid plans and is suddenly met with a brick wall. And because I felt that my body and doctors had failed me, I turned to what any insane person would in moments of sheer panic: www.what-the-frig-do-I-do-now.com.

The following is a list of stuff the internet told me to do to get pregnant:

- Eat healthy food. Check.
- Drink less alcohol. Check.
- Quit coffee. Check.
- Quit dairy. Check.
- Quit gluten. (Dammit!) Check.
- After sex, rest legs against wall. Check.
- Pray. Check.
- Take your temperature with a special, super fancy thermometer the instant you wake up. Check.
- Chart temperature and other fertility signs. (Hello, um, cervix? Are you open? Let me jam my finger up there and...) Check.
- Have sex like crazy within your fertile window, but not too much, because you want quality sperm. Check-ish.
- Keep praying. Check.
- Eat pineapple around ovulation. Check.
- Take maca root supplement. Check.
- Develop a super complicated Traditional Chinese Medicine regimen around supplements and the movement of qi (pronounced "chee"). Checked like a friggin' boss!
- Get acupuncture. Check.
- Put a heating pad on my uterus (but only during certain times of the menstrual cycle or everything—I mean everything—is ruined!). Check.
- Detox. Check.

- Convince husband to detox. Psh! No check.
- Pray some more. Check
- Do yoga. But, embarrassingly, alert the instructor when you're menstruating or ovulating so they don't have you do certain poses. Check.
- After sex, don't move for at least ten minutes. Then get out of bed, turn around three times, do yoga tree pose, break out guitar, sing kumbaya. Just kidding (sort of).
- Use egg whites to mimic cervical mucus. Insert with turkey baster. Check. (I literally would have done anything to get pregnant, can you tell?)
- Perform a vaginal steam routine. Okay, line crossed.

Most of these things were needless, born out of my permeating desperation to create a baby. Had I listened to my gut, I would have stuck with a chosen few, thereby reducing the ensuing panic and frustration after none of them worked. Because when one thing didn't work, I ditched it and went on to the next thing that didn't work until the list was exhausted and I felt more bewildered and desperate than before.

Here's the thing: somewhere along the way I trusted Dr. Google more than I trusted myself. Can you feel the profundity of that statement? I sought and trusted something outside of me to guide me in a major life decision. I hated my body for its betrayal, I didn't trust my doctors, and I sought "expertise" from the abyss of information in hopes that something out there would prove to be the magic pill, exercise, position, substance…anything to help me have a baby. It only served to perpetuate the madness. Had I quieted the desperation, I likely would have heard the whisperings that would have brought me the tranquility I so fervently desired. Instead, I got cerebral. Something that had proven so useful over the last few decades—my ability to think—had not been useful in my pursuit of parenthood. Yet I still attempted to shove that square peg into a round hole. What's the definition of insanity? Doing the same thing over and over and expecting different results. Well, then. It's time to do something different.

Every single time I've asked a client to get quiet with me and notice what they actually want, it's different from what they feel they "should" want. It's different from what their parents want, doctors want, spouse wants, and the rest of the world says they should want. Most of the time, it feels outrageous. It could be something as big as choosing a donor cycle or transferring that mosaic embryo despite the odds against success, or something as simple as (gasp!) saying no to that baby shower invite. (Oh, but it's my sister-in-law; she'll be so offended. So what? She'll live. Probably.) Your greater self always knows better. And so it was with me, as you will find in the coming chapters.

At this point in my journey, however, I was still stuck in the notion that docs know better than me. Thus, I walked into my first RE visit. I can recall that day vividly. I recall driving through the parking lot, walking into the building, looking for the doctor's name on the ledger outside the elevator, getting into the elevator, going up the two flights, and walking into the clinic that would be my home for the next five years—the clinic on which my deepest hopes were resting, where I searched desperately for a friendly face and for someone to tell me that this is where magic happened. I knew one day we'd be bringing my little baby in to take a picture with the doctor who made their conception possible. I can recall the smells in that building, all the noises, the color of the carpet, the fake plants, and the waiting area with the various pamphlets about infertility and financing resources. I can recall gazing down at the floor, wholly embarrassed by my presence there. Even knowing that others were there for the same reason, I couldn't fathom that this was me, that I was actually in a place where I had to get help from a doctor in order to do this very natural thing of conceiving our first child. "Well," I thought, "Thank God we only have to do this once." Ahem.

I felt rather bewildered at that first appointment. For such a personal issue, it all felt extremely impersonal. When my name was called, I jumped what felt like three feet in the air. The nurse was likely used to seeing deer-in-headlights expressions like mine. "Come on back," she said nonchalantly. I followed her down the hall to the blood-draw room, where I got my first blood-draw poke of what seems like thousands (probably hundreds in reality) over the next several years. I remember barely speaking to the phlebotomist because I was still not believing for a second that I was actually in this place. After that momentous blood draw, I was led back to the waiting area, where I waited what seemed an inordinate amount of time for the doctor to show up. If I were a nail-biter, I'm sure my nails would have been down to the cuticles by that point. Instead, I burned a thousand calories shaking my leg and nervously reading through whatever magazines they had there on parenthood and weeknight recipes.

At last I was called back to the RE's office. As I was led down the hall, I was assaulted by large frames of parents and their babies, who had presumably been conceived thanks to this clinic's services. I resented that those photos were there. Like the magazines in the waiting room, they were blunt, painful reminders of all I didn't have. I'm sure they were meant to be inspiring reminders of what could be achieved in that clinic, and nowadays I see the lovingness behind those smiling family photos. At the time, though, I wanted to run away screaming.

Instead, I pretended I was okay and allowed myself to be unceremoniously led into the office of my new RE, whom I shall affectionately refer to as Dr. Pompous. At this juncture, though, I welcomed his know-it-all vibe. I needed a doctor to just tell me what to do. I needed to not have all the answers, and I wanted a physician, a professional, to tell me that they knew exactly what to do and that they could do it in as little time and with as few financial resources as possible. That is precisely what Dr. P said. I was elated and super hopeful for the first time in what felt like years. Quickly, he explained that I was "unexplained" in terms of an infertility diagnosis. All my numbers looked great. My husband had a slight morphology issue, but that was not in itself an issue because it would all be taken care of through the loveliness of science. Though my head was spinning as Dr. P took out his graphs and photos and rates of success and told me precisely how he'd like to proceed in my treatment, I nodded hopefully and brightly with what I'm sure was desperation in my eyes. Dr. P looked quite sure of himself and spoke so quickly, with medical terms I didn't know, that I trusted him implicitly. Thus, we proceeded with our first intrauterine insemination (IUI).

How innocent I was back then. After a BFN (Big Fat Negative) with that IUI, I was floored. With all of Dr. P's confidence, I thought timing everything medically and "washing" T's sperm would prove successful for us. I obsessed daily about having our little baby in my arms. All the while, everything in my universe was pointing to the impossibility of my dreams coming true. I was now more desperate than ever. And what was my go-to when I was desperate? Why, the internet, of course! I searched all kinds of terms, vehemently seeking answers for why our IUI cycle didn't work. "First-time IUI success." "First-time IUI failure." "Why would an IUI cycle fail?" "How can an IUI cycle go wrong?" "What to do after an IUI failure." "How can IUI be improved?" "Whatthefuckhappenedwhydidntthiscycleworkgoddammit!"

So now, based on what you've already learned about what desperation does to the body, what do you think happened to my body after hanging out in desperation mode a while longer? I didn't know it then, but cortisol, adrenaline, inflammation, pain, and headaches were all a product of my desperate thoughts. They were all hanging out as a result of the way I was handling this fertility journey. I was not well. And I would not be well for some time.

Fertility Key: Quiet the Desperation

In the months and years following that initial RE appointment, my body became an inflamed, bruised, and bewildered mess. On one hand, I was trying to make it do something natural; on the other hand, I was feeding it chemicals designed to create more inflammatory mess. Stress hormones and drugs to make my ovaries a hundred times bigger than they're supposed to be? The idea seemed outrageous enough on its own, but on top of that, it also meant that I had to ditch the wine and coffee. The sign hanging in my kitchen says, "Life is what happens between coffee and wine," so you can imagine how much I loved the idea of getting rid of those two elixirs of life! Yet I was desperate to make a baby, so I would have done anything.

My husband, on the other hand, was not as desperate as me. Oh, he wanted a baby, and he wanted a baby badly. But he was able to compartmentalize—to live life sans the insanity of looking for the next saint prayer or blessed water that might make my body do what it was supposed to do. And he absolutely would not agree to a cleanse. He was willing to let it be how it was. In retrospect, I see that my husband had the right idea. My desperation didn't help. In fact, knowing what we now know about the mind-body-spirit connection, I was likely creating more harm than anything else.

I want to help you avoid that mistake. I want to help you let go of the desperation, create peace in your mind and spirit, and create calm in your body.

By calming these essential parts of you, you'll be creating a space that is inviting to your baby. You'll be nurturing a sacred, homey, plush corner for your baby to nestle and grow in. A cup of coffee or a brief run in the neighborhood will not mar the sacredness of this space. On the other hand, a flood of toxic stress hormones will.

When it comes down to it, there are only two basic emotions: fear and love. Desperation comes from fear, and dealing with the fear you likely experience on an hourly basis is the way to calm. Think about the gazelle at the beginning of this chapter. She's desperate to get away from the lion. She feels fear every time the lion comes along. Once the threat is over, however, the fear is gone and she settles. That behavior is the perfect reflection of a healthy mind and body. Were she to hold on to her past (i.e., continue to feel threatened by the lion), she would create chronic desperation showing up as weakness in her mind and body. If she were desperate to get away from the lion, she would have to keep running, even when the lion wasn't present. She may even succumb more readily to the lion the next time it threatened her, because she would have exhausted her resources.

The same goes for you: If you continue to live from fear and desperation, you'll exhaust your resources for when a real threat arises. If, on the other hand, you practice living in the present, you'll enhance your wellness. And if the worst-case scenario does rear its ugly head, you'll be able to handle it with more grace and ease. It will fail to take you down into depression and despair. Do you understand how powerful that makes you? Infertility can cause chaos and disrupt lives, and it may seem like you've lost complete control and have headed down the path of desperation. Yet, through your ability to address the desperation and cultivate calm, you have more control than you ever thought possible. You are powerful. You are wise. And you are calm. Let's look at action steps to help make this your reality.

> **Through your ability to address the desperation and cultivate calm, you have more control than you ever thought possible.**

Action Steps: Notice, Acknowledge, and Calm

Here's where you get to put what you've learned to good, practical use. This and the coming chapters will have specific, useful exercises for you to try out and see how they feel. If you'd like to create your own ninety-day program, take ten days to complete the action steps in each chapter.

Exercises

Each chapter for the rest of this program will have one to three exercises for you to complete so you can learn the Fertility Key well. Some are journal exercises while others are designed to practice with your physical, emotional, or spiritual bodies. In this chapter, I've assigned tasks designed to help you notice your desperate feelings then quietly move them from your experience. The ultimate goal is to calm your body energy enough to create a sense of peace.

Mantra

A mantra is traditionally a word or set of words used to aid concentration in meditation. Words are incredibly powerful. They can elicit a strong biological response, especially depending on the meaning the user gives them. The mantras in this book are designed to elicit a calming or strongly positive response. If at any time you don't feel comfortable with any of the words being used in the mantras, please change them so they do feel comfortable.

Meditation

One of the key processes in transcending infertility is mindfulness meditation. When I began my healing journey, I read about how mindfulness reduces stress—something I desperately needed to do. Nonetheless, I approached meditation with a bit of a smirk. "This is stupid," I thought. "I'm going to prove the research wrong. I mean, I can't meditate! My thoughts are all over the place!" However, nothing else had managed to calm my spirit, so I decided to give it a try, mainly to prove that I was an anomaly—no matter how many people had been helped by meditation, I knew that it wouldn't work for me. I couldn't have been more wrong.

The fact is, meditation—particularly mindfulness meditation—is the number-one reason I feel sane today. I cannot emphasize this enough. Meditation is a giant key to calming the infertility beast and encouraging peace, gratitude, and connection with my spirit. I started small, by paying attention to my breathing. I felt kind of silly at first, sitting there thinking, "Okay, I know I'm breathing. So what?" After a few seconds, my mind would inevitably wander, and I'd find it somewhere in La La Land, thinking about all kinds of things, from scooping dog poop in the backyard to what was on the dinner menu that night. In the beginning, I didn't have the wherewithal to move my mind back to breathing. I was bored. And, truth be told, all the anxiety, anger, sadness, and angst made its way back to the forefront of my mind whenever I meditated. "Great!" I thought. "Not only does meditation not work for me, it's actually making my thoughts worse!"

I didn't realize that accepting that I had a thinking mind (like we all do) is one of the first indications of growth for a new meditator. The next step was to not get agitated when I had thoughts. This step took me what seemed like forever to master. I was super bored and annoyed that my thoughts kept wandering off, and by the second month I was continually scolding myself: "You should know how to do this by now, Maria! What's wrong with you? See? Meditation just doesn't work for you!" Still, I would make it a point to sit and meditate just as I'd planned. I'm not sure where my stubborn streak comes from (I suspect both of my parents), but it came in handy as day after day I sat to meditate— refusing to give up, slowly moving toward day 90 when I could claim that I was right and meditation didn't work for me.

It was during the second month of meditation that I began to notice a change in myself. Topics related to pregnancy and parenthood still annoyed me significantly. Other things, though—like people cutting me off on the highway—were only minor offenses in my mind. Historically, I would muster up my best Jersey Girl, flash my high beams, honk my horn, and scream at the top of my lungs at the offensive idiot who dared get in front of me in my lane.

I would speed up and try to catch the son of a bitch's eye just to feel the satisfaction of flipping him a stiff bird. By the second month of meditation, I considered the same experience a mere blip on my radar. In fact, I began thinking, "Hey, you never know. The guy could be having a heart attack and need to get to a hospital soon." Who the hell was I? Strangely enough, I didn't attribute these changes to meditation at first. I don't know what I thought, though I suspect I thought the fertility drugs were finally out of my system, not even stored in my fat anymore. Whatever the case, I was intrigued by this new, calmer version of myself. By the end of the third month, I noticed an even more significant change in myself. I'd always claimed to be a relatively rosy person with a great outlook on life, but this went even beyond rosy. I saw glimpses of friggin' Mother Theresa, who noted she saw "Jesus in all of His distressing disguises."

You'll learn in the coming chapters specifically how important meditation is in your journey to parenthood. This and all following Action segments will end with a meditation specifically designed to help create new synaptic connections in your brain after repeated use. We're looking to create new neuronal pathways in your brain—literally rewiring your brain—so that you consciously create your future rather than creating the same past reality over and over.

Each guided meditation is designed to be listened to, so when the time comes, please go to www.drmariarothenburger.com/transcendingmeditations, where you can listen to the meditations pre-recorded by yours truly. Meditation is important for transcending infertility, so don't skip it!

Exercise 1: Notice the Desperation

Your very first move in this Action Step is to simply notice the desperation you have on a daily basis. The goal here is to get a good baseline of where your current desperation is, so you can gauge progress in the future.

For this exercise, get out your journal. Create a page where you track how many times per day you search something related to your fertility. There's no need to change how often you search just yet. The goal at this juncture is to simply be mindful of how much time you're spending in the desperate space of looking for answers, checking statistics, looking up treatments, and wondering what others' symptoms are and whether they had successful cycles.

Just notice. Write it down. I recommend doing this exercise for at least three days to get a decent baseline read on how often you follow through on the desperate impulse for information.

Write down how many minutes/hours you spend researching fertility-related items daily.

Exercise 2: Quiet the Desperation

After you have a good baseline reading of what you're doing on the internet for a few days, your next move is to get into a calm state of mind. There are several ways you can begin doing this. I'm not asking you to quit Dr. Google cold turkey; I'm merely asking that you begin to consider reducing the amount of time you obsessively check on a day-to-day basis. Getting your brain used to reducing the urge to check will increase your tolerance to the impulse, and eventually you'll begin to realize how unimportant most of the searches are.

Consider implementing one of the following things. You don't need to implement them all. In fact, if you decide you're going to do them all and do them perfectly as if part of a checklist, you're likely operating from a space of desperation. Choose at least one of them, with the main focus being ease, intention, and utter imperfection. If you get any of these right 30% of the time, you're golden.

Social Media & Internet Searches

Schedule your social media and Google time. This might seem weird. "Shouldn't I just not do internet searches or be on social media at all?" you may be asking. That is not what I recommend. Here's the thing: internet and social media become like a drug. Our brains literally get used to doing the same thing over and over, and we create habits. Before we know it, it feels weird to not do that habit, and we must do it again in order to create a sense of homeostasis. To that end, what I'm asking you to do seems counterintuitive. I'm asking you to do the equivalent of drinking one cup of coffee a day rather than completely obliterating all signs of caffeine from your body. I don't want to create headaches from the withdrawal. I want to help you cut back while also offering the satisfaction of a warm cup o' joe (or Google) within reason.

Now, how do you schedule your internet time? Let me be completely vague for a moment and say, it depends. I once worked with someone who admitted she was internet searching for eight hours a day. Others search for two or three hours a day, spread out over the entire day. There are two things I'd like you to ask yourself:

1. How much time on the internet feels better to me (enough to make me feel in control and not overwhelmed)?
2. How much less can I do tomorrow?

Once you've answered these questions, schedule your Google time in the following way:

Tomorrow, I will search the internet to my heart's desire for _____ minutes less than I did today, which is _____ (total amount of time). I will continue to reduce daily until I have reached my baseline goal of _____ (maximum amount of time you want to spend on the internet/social media).

Then follow through! After a few weeks of this, you'll be shocked at how much calmer you feel. Or, if my intuition is right, you won't be shocked, because you already know that internet searches and social media don't serve you well right now.

Create a Brain Dump

In the beginning of slowing down and retraining your brain to remove addiction to internet searches, the withdrawal will likely be difficult, even though I'm encouraging you to do this incrementally. So, I recommend creating a page in your journal—or perhaps a note on your phone—for a "Brain Dump." I love my Brain Dump space so much, it's several pages long after only a few months of use.

A Brain Dump space is a place where you can write down all your impulses in order to get them out of your head. Like that one time I just had to know how to get to Seattle by way of Amtrak but had no way to search. Oh no! What's a girl to do? Enter the Brain Dump. I happen to have a dedicated space in my Bullet Journal (www.bulletjournal.com), but any way you organize yourself will do. Perhaps a voice note or typed note on your phone? A text to yourself? Post-its? A notebook? An email to yourself? A space in your journal? It doesn't matter how you Brain Dump, it only matters that you do.

Now, what does one do with the Brain Dump? I recommend regularly checking your Brain Dump for actually important items to research during the time you've allotted to research. If you've given yourself ten hours of research in a day, the first source of things to research is your Brain Dump. Here's what's cool about looking there first: You may find that many things are irrelevant now, and you've likely saved yourself a ton of time avoiding the rabbit hole of research by simply writing it down, delaying research gratification, and marking it irrelevant a few days later. I didn't really need to research Amtrak tickets right then, as we plan to go six months from now. On my Brain Dump list it went, and eventually it will make it to my bullet journal task list for the month. Some things make it on my Brain Dump list and never end up on a task list, because they are irrelevant for my life. I've saved myself a ton of time by doing this.

The Brain Dump has two significant benefits:

1. It helps create impulse control. (No more random "Hey, Siri" in the middle of breakfast with your loved one. Don't think I didn't notice that!)
2. It saves you mega time by reducing the impulse to research immediately.

It's worth it. Set it up now.

Plan for Fun

Admit it. You haven't been having fun lately. Between doctor's visits, work, social functions, and buying new clothes to fit your IVF bloat, who can blame you? If you really think about it, because of all the above—and a million other things you do that aren't mentioned—you deserve some fun. Not only do you deserve it, it's essential.

I want you to take out your calendar right now and look at some days and times when you can plan to have some fun. When was the last time you felt truly peaceful or had a huge belly laugh that you almost couldn't stop? If you can't remember, it's been far too long. The plan here is to obliterate all those stress chemicals floating around in your bloodstream and replace them with some feel-good chemicals designed for wellness.

Write your top five things that feel peaceful to you and/or elicit belly laughs:

1.

2.

3.

4.

5.

Pick one you can do in the next week and schedule it in (remaining flexible, of course). Pick one you can do in the next two weeks. Schedule it. And so on. I'd like to see your calendar having at least three truly peaceful or laughter-inducing plans for the next ninety days.

Fertility Mantra

Write down these words and put them in a place where you'll see them daily. Take slow breaths (inhale to the count of five and exhale to the count of five). Practice this mantra twice a day. I like to tie these to things you already do twice a day, such as brushing your teeth. You choose. Now, slow your breathing and say these words out loud or in your mind:

Breathing In: I am calm

Breathing Out: I am smiling

Breathing In: I am peaceful

Breathing Out: I am smiling

(Repeat three times.)

Fertility Meditation: Quieting the Desperation

I've already mentioned this: Do not skip this part. I should probably consider creating the meditation police, but that would likely be contrary to the point. Alas, I shall honor you and all you choose to do. But seriously, don't skip this.

Do this meditation daily for the next ten days. (Reminder: you can access my recordings of this and all other meditations from this book at www.drmariarothenburger.com/transcendingmeditations.)

Lying down or sitting in a comfortable position, closing your eyes gently, begin paying attention to your breath. Inhale, exhale. Inhale, exhale.

Imagine now, with every exhale you are breathing out the stresses in your body. And with every inhale, you're able to take in all the peacefulness surrounding you.

Inhale, exhale. Inhale, exhale.

Noticing your feet now. Clench up your feet as small as they will go, hold—two, three, four—and release. Inhale, exhale. Now your calves: Clench them up tightly. Hold—two, three, four—and release. Inhale and exhale. And your thighs: Hold—two, three, four—and release. Inhale, exhale.

Moving up to your abdomen, holding it in as tightly as you can. Holding—two, three, four—and release. Inhale and exhale. And now your shoulders, tightening them up and holding for one, two, three, four—and release them all the way loose.

Noticing now the muscles of your face and your neck. Tighten them up as tight as they will go; hold for one, two, three, four—and release them all the way relaxed. Noticing that even the muscles behind your eyes have relaxed greatly. Feeling the surface beneath you, whether it is the floor or a bed, and noticing that it is fully supporting your body as you melt into it. Fully trusting you will be held and supported in all your relaxation.

And now imagine a healing light above you. It can be whatever color you choose, a color that holds significant healing meaning for you. This light creates a sense of peace within you and is there to remind you that you are safe, you are loved, and all is exactly as it should be.

Imagine the light moving into your head space now. It lights up your brain and all the fluids within. It travels down through your neck into your spinal cord, all the way down into your feet, lighting up every bone, soft tissue, artery, and capillary along the way.

Breathing in, breathing out. This light is like a loving presence or hug. A presence that fills you with peace, with tranquility. Breathing in, breathing out.

Circling back up your body now, the light travels toward your heart. This is where the light becomes extremely bright. With every pump of your heart, the light is sent throughout all your veins to nourish the rest of your body with its healing presence.

Feeling peaceful, easy, light, and totally relaxed, this light creates a sense that you need not worry about next steps in your journey.

Breathing in, breathing out…

Inhaling peace, exhaling stress…

The light is in your heart, guiding you, reminding you of its wisdom. Moving from your headspace into your heart will always steer you in the healthy, wise direction.

Just being with this light now…

Inhaling, exhaling. Noticing the light filtering through your entire body, encompassing it in its healing glow.

Letting go of any worry, desperation, heaviness, and doubt about the future now. Breathing it all out. Replacing every bit of angst with the light's wisdom.

You are safe. You are whole. You are peaceful and quiet, and you move through your journey with ease.

And so it is.

What's Next?

When you calm down and arrive at a less desperate place, a shift happens. You're able to pay more attention to the things happening around us. You may even become more aware of difficult thoughts and emotions; this is normal. And the rest of this book will aid in moving through those difficult moments. Interactions with ourselves and others become more pronounced somehow, and we begin noticing things we may not have paid much attention to while in fight-or-flight mode.

One such behavior is pretending. We tend to put on a happy face and act as if all is well, right? We do this at baby showers, at weddings, at first birthday parties, and when visiting a friend or relative and their new baby in the hospital. We pretend while in public, and sometimes we pretend in private. I call this "wearing an infertility mask." Sometimes all this faking becomes painful, doesn't it? It begins to stifle who we really are in our current experiences.

The next chapter is a story of my own masks, how I wore them, and what happened when I took them off (hint: everyone lived). You'll learn about your own masks and will find balance between protecting yourself with a mask and safely being your true unmasked self.

Chapter Three

Wearing Infertility Masks

To thine own self be true.
— William Shakespeare

Have you ever heard the notion "fake it till you make it?" It's actually a pretty big concept in the therapy world, specifically in Cognitive Behavioral Therapy where one simply tells oneself a completely different thought than the one hanging out in the head. For example, the thought "I'm an idiot; I can't do anything right" becomes "I'm smart; I can do a lot of things right." Now, in principal, I can understand why this type of therapy works (and it does work—lots of research to back that up). Basically, every thought produces a chemical. And if that chemical matches depression and/or anxiety, one will feel depressed and/or anxious. Conversely, if the thought matches gratitude, happiness, or contentment, the associated chemical will produce said emotional states. This is, of course, a rather simplified explanation.

Generally, when people are trying to conceive, they cannot magically and instantaneously be pregnant by the thought "I am pregnant." Herein lies the struggle with this medical condition. The thought "I am pregnant" may actually be quite triggering for the trauma and cause *more* of the unwanted chemical state. Yikes! We've already gone over what those negative chemicals do to fertility. Let's not encourage that, shall we? What if the thought is "I'm going to be pregnant one day"? Still triggering? What if the thought is "I'm hopeful this is all going to work out"? Less triggering?

Here's the thing: the thought doesn't matter as much as how you *feel* about it. The environment around you doesn't matter as much to your fertility as how you *feel* about it. The thought "I am pregnant" could be a wonderful, pleasant thought to one person and entirely painful to another. You have ultimate control! You have ultimate choice! That's what you're after while dealing with fertility struggles, right? One caveat is that sometimes faking is useful. It keeps us safe when we're absolutely beyond-words hurting. It's the cave in which we retreat to lick our wounds, and there's nothing wrong with that. The key here is that the retreat is authentically pleasing to you. One time I decided to take my infertility mask off and be obnoxious during a baby shower. Probably not my greatest moment. I made everyone uncomfortable, including myself. It would have been more useful and pleasing to me (and everyone) to don my mask and cry when I got home ("Why yes, that onesie is cute, but yours is epic!" Drive home. Cue waterfall of tears.).

Other times, faking is not useful, and authentic expression of one's true self is paramount. This chapter will help you learn the difference. Following is a story during our journey that required ultimate authentic self-expression. I didn't even know I needed to be authentic, and from then on, I gave myself permission to be just that.

Masks

Years ago, while I sat alone in my one-bedroom apartment, being introspective and quiet—a true introvert—my serenity was marred by the ringing of the telephone. I got up in a huff to check the caller ID (I know; I'm totally dating myself here). To my delight, it was my sister, D. I love D. She's like a breath of fresh air or, more accurately, a dose of reality when I'm caught up in my own shit. D is the person who will kindly tell you if your pants make you look fat. You can count on it. She's awesome.

Though we grew up together, we hadn't lived near each other for five or six years at that point. By the age of sixteen, the roughness of D's black-sheep wool had chafed Mom's top layer of skin right off, and D moved out with a boyfriend, got her GED, and began living. Eventually she made her way to the northwest, where she regretted living with our dad and brother yet also felt at home with the life and culture. She married at twenty and struggled in that relationship. The last I'd heard, there had been some infidelity, and divorce was on the table. So when the caller ID displayed her number, I thought she wanted to talk the marriage issues out with me. Man, was I in for a surprise. I know what you're thinking: No, she wasn't pregnant. After the usual hello-how-are-yous, our conversation went something like this:

D: So…I have something to tell you.
Me: Okaaayyy.
D: Um. Don't judge me, 'kay?
Me: Okay!
D: I think I've known for a long time that, well…I think I'm gay.
Me: Oh! Okay, that's cool.
D: It is?
Me: Yeah! You're still my sister.
D: Yep.

And that was that. We talked more about her coming out and how her life would change, etc., but never in a billion years did it occur to me that she was somehow different or "less than." For what probably seemed a billion years to her, D had worn a mask. She pretended to be who she perceived a girl should be instead of owning her authentic, messy beauty. She made nice, dated guys, married a guy, and played with makeup, all the while pretending to be amused when someone called her a tomboy. She did manage, however, to totally avoid dresses at all costs.

Ripping that mask off must have been so freeing! To think of it now, I feel physically lighter—like dancing on a mountain, singing about the hills being alive. Yet the sheer terror of vulnerability must have been acutely present as well. There is so much possibility for judgment, opinions, anger, and offensiveness, as if the mere glance of a gay person could burn one's skin to a crisp. Perhaps the most significant player in all the judgment on D was our mom. It wasn't that rejection from others didn't hurt, but history informed the already-present divide between D and Mom. You know, black sheep's wool and all. In short, Mom truly loves D. D truly loves Mom. Mom's version of what should make D happy is different from what actually makes D happy. Voila! Divide. It doesn't take a therapist to figure that out.

Flash forward to my particularly dark state of infertility. One day while I was milling around with T at Bed Bath & Beyond, ostensibly to buy a gift, I looked up to see a baby store—marked by enormous, colorful, and achingly joyous letters announcing "you don't belong here" via B-A-B-I-E-S in its title. It was the store next door, and I had noticed it, of course, along with at least five pregnant bellies assaulting my muted world of depression and constant brain fog. To me, baby stores were like sunlight to a vampire. Except I didn't get that cool sparkly skin effect like in that one vampire movie. Rather, it burned. And as I perused the vegetable peelers, I couldn't shake the dark cloud taunting me with its damp fullness, ready to dump buckets of rain on my fragile ego at any moment.

Like always, I pretended all was well. I'd occasionally smile at a fellow patron as if I, too, coveted that amazing salad spinner. But after years of shielding my inner world from the masses, I felt my proverbial mask starting to crack. I wonder now if that's what D experienced just before revealing her true self.

Thankfully, the phone rang, snapping me out of my weird misty mind. So different from the slight annoyance I'd felt that time when my sister interrupted my introspection, I hungrily fished the phone out of my bag and saw that it was Mom. I happily answered, eager for some refuge from my triggered world, when I realized she was very upset. It was about D. Months prior, D had come out of the closet, and Mom was still reeling and praying for her every day to be healed from this condition. By the time she called me, she was tipping precariously over the edge of sanity. I totally related. Mom described an argument she and D had about D being gay and how Mom would never accept it. I compassionately listened as best I could. All my training had surfaced: active listening, asking for clarification, blah blah blah. I was putting all my energy into helping someone else when I hadn't put the proverbial oxygen mask on myself yet.

Suddenly, I felt it. The crack in my infertility mask began as a mere hairline fracture, but it rapidly began resembling the deep fissures of the Grand Canyon. I looked at T with an expression only he would understand. He nodded, and I bolted. I ran for the car with not so much as a glance at the stupid baby-store sign looming over me. All the while, Mom kept talking about the argument and how upset she was and how she feared she'd never talk to her daughter again because "she'll never change." I couldn't take it anymore. The swell of tears came out. Mom said, "Don't cry, or you'll make me cry." It was way too late for that. At that point, the infertility beast was about to surface. Compassionate understanding and the I've-got-this-I'm-a-therapist persona flew out the window. What I wanted to say was, "Fuck this, fuck this stupid-ass situation, what the fuck are you talking about, this fucking sucks, fuck fuck fuck!" Fortunately, I hadn't yet had wine that day, so what came out instead was marginally better.

Through a torrent of tears and hiccups, I said, "I wish you could understand. Here I am striving, wishing, begging, yearning for the baby I can't have, and you're rejecting one of the precious ones you already have! Do you even have the slightest idea how lucky you are? If a baby were dropped on my doorstep—an alien with green skin and purple spots, gay or straight—I would love, accept, and appreciate that soul for all he or she is and never look back for a solitary second. Please don't do this, Mom. She needs you."

We both paused. I'd like to believe Mom was thinking, "Holy shit. She's right." But I really don't know. We didn't dive any deeper into feelings that day because, honestly, I'm a recovering stoic. (I was also raised by one—ahem…thanks, Mom?) Also, I was reeling from having my mask fall off. The carefully guarded gaping wounds were now wide open—and so was my jaw! I wondered at this new version of my sordid self—the self that was vulnerable, authentic, dark, broken. I was fully exposed. I did not have my shit together. And I was at once perplexed, relieved, and terrified.

Overall, it felt good. I don't recall how that conversation ended, but ten years later, D and Mom have the best relationship they've ever had. D still hates dresses. Sometimes Mom calls her a tomboy. It's all good.

My Infertility Mask

Neither my mom nor my sister knew what I was going through. I wore my infertility mask like a friggin' champ; at least I thought I did. Nobody knew that I was desperately hopeful every time I went to the acupuncturist's office, even when he told me to ingest those dastardly herbs meant to improve hormonal function. (Holy crap! I still have the aftertaste in my mouth all these years later!) Nobody knew of my efforts to get my fertility yoga moves just right or that I beat myself up when my body couldn't quite get into all those awesome poses. If they'd seen all the supplement bottles lined up on my counter, expertly numbered and arranged based on the precise part of my menstrual cycle, I imagine they would have stared in open-mouthed awe at my organizational skills.

After many moons of trying to conceive with Eastern medicine and other such avenues post-IUI, T and I decided to move on to in vitro fertilization (IVF). Now, the media would have you believe that IVFs are one-and-done. "If you can't get pregnant, go get yourself some IVF, and voila! Diapers, breastfeeding, sleep deprivation, and cute little onesies will take over your life just as you've always wanted! It's so easy!" Ha! Just getting through the how-the-heck-are-we-going-to-pay-for-this part was an astounding hurdle. I'll spare you the details, as I think it's beyond the scope of this book. Suffice it to say that, as of the date of this writing, there aren't enough states mandating infertility coverage and there are enough loopholes that insurance companies are able to not-so-stealthily slide by the very real need for this coverage. T's insurance covered $4,000 for a lifetime, and my insurance covered $0. For a lifetime. Were insurance companies covering more infertility treatment, they would save a heck of a lot more in mental and other health-condition payouts because the stress of infertility leads directly to health decline. Period. Stepping down from soapbox now.

Okay, so where was I? Ah yes, our first IVF. Such a beautiful dream. Thanks to social media, I believed that almost everyone in treatment conceived on their first IVF cycle, so as long as we could gather the funds, we would have our baby within the next year. I was hopeful yet still extremely stressed out. This was $15,000 on the line—money that, frankly, we didn't have, money we had to borrow. In hindsight, I still would've done the same thing; a baby is totally worth it. However, the decision is not without stress. Once finances were secured, we were ready to move on to our first IVF cycle. We were sure it was going to work, and we were excited.

One of my healthy infertility masks was the use of humor, and I recall drawing this series of IVF events leading up to the conclusion of this first cycle.

Holy meds, Batman!

Wow. That needle prick wasn't so bad.

Number two prick, done! This is easy!

Great. Cute pregnant woman. Ouch, my ovaries hurt.

This is harder now.

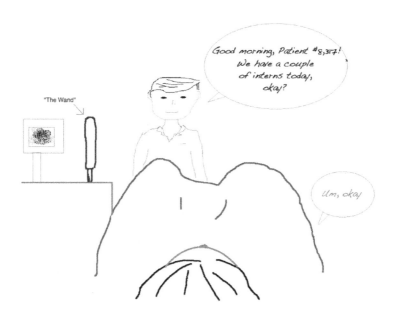

"Good morning, Patient #8,317. We have a couple of interns today, okay?"
"Um, okay."

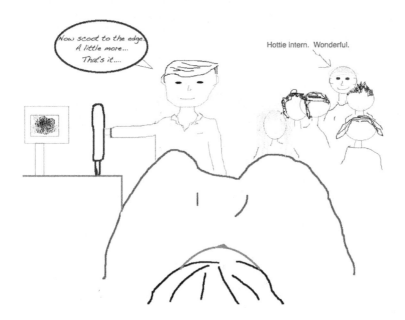

"Now scoot to the edge a little more. That's it."
Hot intern. Ugh.

Jeans held together by a safety pin due to melon-sized ovaries.
This is beginning to suck.

"IVF bloat" as I walked past the new baby consignment shop in my 'hood. Fantastic.

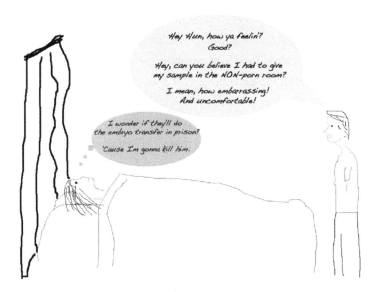

After the egg retrieval:
T: "Can you believe I had to give my sample in the non-porn room? How embarrassing and uncomfortable!"
Me: "I wonder if they'll do the embryo transfer in prison. 'Cause I'm gonna kill him."

Just like most things in my life, I wanted every single step of this IVF process to be perfect. And when it wasn't, I freaked the fuck out. On the other hand, T was like an ol' pro with mixing our stimulation medication. I remember trying to do it myself and shaking like a leaf from all the adrenaline in my system. I finally acquiesced and gave the little vials to him. There were two kinds of meds to mix, and I watched him do it like no big deal. Even injecting my belly was no big deal. It was a teeny-tiny insulin needle and went in with nary a pinch. I couldn't have imagined that those tiny little needles could cause so much bruising. But there was much worse to come.

After that first injection, I woke up in the wee hours of the morning in a panic. I had an intuition that we had mixed the wrong medications. We were supposed to have one vial of medication A and three vials of medication B. I jumped out of bed and dashed downstairs with my heart pounding like I was being chased by a lion. I was a madwoman in PJs, digging through the kitchen garbage, searching incessantly for those four little vials. I found medication A. Okay, that's good. Next vial: Medication B. Okay, so whatever the next one was would tell me the outcome of my search. Found the next vial: Medication A. Holy shit! I had mixed up the medication! I gave T three of medication A and one of medication B! I was on the phone immediately to the nurse with my mind spinning, thinking I had surely caused a cycle disruption and the whole thing would need to be canceled. If I wasn't perfect, disaster was surely on its way.

Frustratingly, I received a voicemail instead of a real person and left my freaked-out, semi-yelling message and nervously awaited a phone call back. A few hours later, the nurse called back and said that I shouldn't worry, that it would all work itself out in the end. "I mean, don't do that again, but it'll be okay." Ha! You'd better believe I would never, ever do that again! After all, I was on my way to a perfect cycle that ended in a baby.

Yet, it wasn't to be. After my first few days on stimulation medication, Dr. P realized my numbers weren't growing the way he expected them to, so I had to increase my dose. "That's all right, doc. It only means a thousand extra dollars. Pocket change, right?" After a few days on the higher dose, my body was like, "Whaaaaaat are you doing to me?" and promptly sent my number skyrocketing such that the doc seemed to shift slightly from his I-know-everything pedestal—a shift that, for me, was quite unsettling. I was advised to stop all medications immediately, and I would have to "coast" for a while before I could take the shot that would trigger ovulation. Meanwhile, my ovaries were the size of small watermelons.

I have a pretty decent pain tolerance, but I was quite annoyed by the fact that I looked five months pregnant and had to hold my pants together with safety pins. The irony was not lost on me by any stretch. Finally, after five freaking days of coasting, while picking at a Greek salad in a noisy mall sitting across from T, I received the call I'd been eagerly awaiting: the RE's office delivering the blessed message that T could issue the trigger shot that night. We were elated! We went in shortly thereafter to have all my glorious eggs surgically removed from my ovaries. It was honestly no big deal. I had been under anesthesia many times prior to that, and I was happy to finally have my ovaries go back down to their normal size.

We had nine eggs retrieved, eight of which were mature. At the time, I thought those numbers were quite low, especially given the size of my ovaries. Dr. P, however, thought that number was glorious, and I decided to trust him—a decision undoubtedly influenced by the fact that I was still only half aware due to the delight that is waking up from anesthesia and finally feeling a bit peaceful. After three days in the embryologist's lab, we had five little embryos and planned to transfer two. Hindsight and a lot of medical changes since then tells me transferring two was not a great idea, but again, I trusted Dr. P.

On the day of transfer, I felt quite unwell. I still looked pregnant, my ovaries were painful, and I simply did not feel right. I didn't know I should report this to my nurse or doc, as I simply thought that was how IVF went. I didn't complain. I was wearing my infertility mask. All was well. Right? Right?!

About three days later, I thought I might have a problem. My abdomen was still very large, I wasn't urinating a whole lot, I was in a lot of pain, and it took effort just to lie down on the couch to watch TV. I recall one lovely evening when T was folding laundry, upset that I wasn't helping him. I wanted to punch him, like those stupid baby photos at the RE's office. The truth is, I even wore my infertility mask around T, and he really didn't know how much pain I was in. He didn't know it hurt to breath. He didn't know I was dizzy every waking moment and that to touch my abdomen would have sent me into a tailspin. So when I suggested I needed to go to the RE's office because I wasn't feeling well, he said, "Okay, I'll see you later," and I drove myself. Had I taken off my infertility mask with the one person whom I needed to trust in this world, I suspect that interaction would have looked a wee bit different. Instead, I huffed and puffed in the car, annoyed that he hadn't offered to take me. I never reminded myself that I hadn't asked him to take me, nor had I told him what bad shape I was in. It was my fault. Stupid infertility mask.

When I got to the RE's office, the (very pregnant, mind you) doctor on call confirmed a diagnosis of Ovarian Hyper-stimulation Syndrome (OHSS). OHSS is a result of overstimulated ovaries (hello—like in all IVF cycles) where there's decreased output of fluid, weight gain (due to fluid), dizziness, nausea, and swelling. Well, no wonder I was suffering so much! I was directed to drink more fluids with electrolytes and monitor my urine output over the next few days with a urine "hat." Even at work. I carried my urine hat down the hall to the ladies' room with a stealth I had never before pulled off. I don't know whether anyone ever saw me carry that thing to and from the restroom, and I'm content to believe that nobody ever did. Back then, my infertility-masked self would proclaim it to be "no big deal" and just a part of this whole process. Inside, however, I was thinking, "Because having a wand shoved up my vagina every couple of days, getting shot in the ass, and looking pregnant when I'm not isn't enough, right? I have to be mortified with a urine hat. Awesome."

When I left the doctor's office that day, the nurse said to me, "Well, congratulations. I've been doing this a long time, and I've never had a case of OHSS end up not pregnant." The urine hat was a small thing when I recalled that moment. This was going to work! The day we got the phone call was a good one; we had both worked all day with no phone message to listen to, and we were watching TV in our family room when the phone rang. We were sure it was good news. I was a staunch no-POASer (pee-on-a-stick-er; I refused to do a home pregnancy test), so we truly did not know what the results would be and fully expected good news.

The nurse's tone of voice was all I registered. I don't recall her words except to say we should schedule a follow-up meeting with our doc to figure out next steps. We were not pregnant. My heart sank, and I looked at T with an expression that I'm sure could break a thousand hearts. When I hung up the phone, I did not emote right away. Slowly, the realization of what had just happened sank in, and I began to feel all the stages of grief in what seemed like a millisecond: denial, anger, bargaining, depression, acceptance. I felt them all at once, then each of them, then all at once, over and over for what seemed an eternity.

> The realization of what had just happened sank in, and I began to feel all the stages of grief in what seemed like a millisecond: denial, anger, bargaining, depression, acceptance.

At that point, my infertility mask was torn off and every raw part of me was exposed. I yelled, I cried, I threw shit, I lay shaking on the bed, I hit walls, I rolled around in a daze, I screamed. All manner of expression came out in those first few hours after that phone call. I was a mess, and I wasn't hiding it. T was a champ. I wrote in my dissertation dedication that T was never one to pull me up out of the darkness. He was the one who climbed down into the darkness and just held me. That's what he did then. When I had settled a bit, wiped away the tears and snot, and was able to breathe a bit better, T tried to comfort me with words.

"It's going to be okay, hun. We've been through harder times, and in the end, everything is going to turn out fine." I didn't believe him. I don't think he believed himself. We were swimming in a sea of brokenness, expectation, and fear of the future. My body felt like it had been hit by a truck, and I don't know that he quite understood that part. I was not myself. I walked the earth in a daze over the coming months. We had just spent $15,000 dollars we didn't have, hoping for a small chance at making our dream come true. Was it worth it? Even as I write this, ten years later, it was worth every penny. It just hurt like hell that we were on the losing end of that bet. And the hell we were feeling was replete with uncertainty about our future and whether we'd be parents.

Because I wore my infertility masks well in most moments, other people didn't know just how sad I was. They knew I was different, that I had gained weight, that I was avoidant, isolative, and downright irritable. What they didn't know is that I was in a deep, resonant depression. I couldn't escape the despondency. I had lost my peppy, cheerful, optimistic spirit, and I no longer recognized the person looking back at me in the mirror. They also didn't know that as I drove home every day, merely stopping at traffic lights would elicit traumatic sensations of feeling stymied, held back, forcefully paused on the way to my destination.

> Because I wore my infertility masks well in most moments, other people didn't know just how sad I was. They knew I was different, that I had gained weight, that I was avoidant, isolative, and downright irritable. What they didn't know is that I was in a deep, resonant depression. I couldn't escape the despondency. I had lost my peppy, cheerful, optimistic spirit, and I no longer recognized the person looking back at me in the mirror.

Depression also has a lovely way of numbing pain at times, so when I wasn't freaked out, I was merely curious. I would have extremely difficult thoughts, cock my head, and think, "I wonder where that came from?" Then I would move on with my gray existence, see clients, write notes, smile when I was supposed to, nod when the moment allowed, and drive back home to be in the emptiness residing there. I ate, took showers, did laundry, and sometimes cleaned. All the while, I felt like a robot. I don't know if even T saw it; I was already dying inside.

Over the next few months, T and I had more conversations about what to do next. We decided to follow up with the infamous WTF doc appointment (where you sit with your doc and figure out what may have gone wrong and what to do next). Dr. P presented with a bit more humility at this office visit. T and I sat obligingly as Dr. P went over what he thought may have been better and what we could do for the next cycle. "Next cycle?" I thought. "How in the world are we going to fund that monster bill?" As Dr. P announced that he thought we should move forward with another cycle, that often people don't get pregnant after their first cycle, blah blah blah, I began hearing him like an adult in the Peanuts cartoons. He wasn't answering the fundamental question: What the fuck went wrong?

The truth is, he didn't know. And in hindsight, there's no way a doctor can know what goes wrong. They simply do what they can based on their training and insights. I was a desperate woman, wearing my infertility mask, nodding, smiling, saying, "Okay, doc, I see. Um, hmm. I get it. Okay, so we should cycle again? Okay, I see." I likely missed many questions that day because I was trying to be a good patient, not rock the boat, move on from the $15,000 loss.

Dr. P mentioned that he saw the tiniest anomaly on my HSG X-ray and wanted to have a closer look. "What do you think about an exploratory surgery?" In truth, I don't think Dr. P saw a dang thing, and he was merely saying he saw something so that insurance would pay for the exploratory surgery. Bless him. It's the one thing I can honestly say I am so grateful for.

Months later, T and I showed up at the hospital so the doc could see what was going on with my internal lady parts. I nodded groggily as Dr. P explained what he saw while I was blissfully unaware under anesthesia. I haven't the foggiest idea what in the world he said except for four words: *endometriosis*, *uterine scarring*, and *perplexed*. To this day, *perplexed* still rings in my ear when talking about the uterine scarring. I have absolutely no idea where that would have come from; neither did Dr. P. That did not help to assuage my nervous mind.

The next day, I learned more about this whole endometriosis thing. I'd been diagnosed with Stage II endometriosis, a condition where the endometrial lining grows outside of the uterus. It inflames and bleeds just like uterine tissue inside the uterus on a regular basis, and it can cause scarring and incredible pain. "Well, gee, doc, do you think that's why I've had extremely painful periods since I was like fourteen years old? Hmmmm…"

"Yes," Dr. P said. "You've likely had this for a while, and it likely runs in your family. Do you know of anyone else with it?" I know my sister tried to get pregnant before she and her husband split, and I know it took my mom a long while to conceive, even though she was in her early twenties. No wonder my mom thought I was exaggerating how painful my periods were; she thought that was normal, too!

So, what does a fertility patient do when a new diagnosis has been found? You already know the answer, right? Dr. Google! I researched and researched and researched. The research and medical information stated that endometriosis was incurable. Bleak. I found that some doctors believed an autoimmune condition could be the cause of endometriosis, and this gave me a sliver of hope. Even though Dr. P supposedly removed all the adhesions and scarring, I was focused on preventing a reoccurrence of the condition, since it wasn't curable. I immediately made an appointment with Dr. P to talk about IVIg, a controversial treatment some REs were using to treat endometriosis when there was a high number of natural killer cells found in the uterus.

I should have known this meeting was not going to go well. Dr. P was conservative, to say the least. As we were walking into his office, I noted on the office door an article about how bogus acupuncture is for fertility. Those precise words weren't part of the article, of course; however, everything in me resisted the notion that acupuncture is not a viable, beneficial practice for those trying to conceive, and hackles were raised from that point on. What would Dr. P think of IVIg? I delicately brought up the notion of treating the endometriosis as an immune issue, and Dr. P effectively scolded me. Really. I felt like a small child. He schooled me on the fact that some "quack" docs were collecting thousands of dollars for this treatment when it was preposterous, ineffective, and a complete waste of time. When I asked if he'd even be willing to give it a try, Dr. P almost kicked me out of his office. T and I sat frozen as Dr. P offered to send me on my way with the name of a different doctor who could potentially help us. I was floored at his vehemence.

I should have said my goodbyes at that point and calmly walked out, knowing that this was not my doc. But I didn't. Instead, when met with that all-important question—Trust myself or trust the doc?—I acquiesced. I dutifully donned my infertility mask, listened to Dr. P, and did what I was told. Like a "good" fertility patient, I began to plan everything around an IVF cycle, which is essentially the second job I never wanted and, incidentally, one that I had to pay to have—which now meant scrounging up another $15,000! Little did I know how the impact of the emotional, psychological, physical, and spiritual damage of infertility and all its masks were about to catapult me into a spinning world of depression, anxiety, anger, grief, and perpetual trauma. After several years of not being able to be myself, my psyche was becoming threadbare. I was on dangerously thin ice, and it was starting to crack under my feet.

In some ways, I welcomed crashing through the ice into the enveloping, abysmal darkness below; I imagined being enfolded into an arctic comfort. A blast of more pain, then sleep. Gentle, peaceful sleep. The other, very tiny, part of me was terrified of the breaking ice and desperately hoped for the ability to magically float above it. That minuscule part of me hoping to float was my legitimate self. She was the one who knew that all this pain was a mere mirage, and the path to freedom was in and around me. She was compassion, love, warmth, gentleness, and contentment. I needed to access her right then. I needed to hear her clarity, her guidance. But she spoke too softly. I wasn't hearing her through my joyless existence. What I needed was a scream.

> **My legitimate self knew that all this pain was a mere mirage, and the path to freedom was in and around me.**

Fertility Key: Ditch the Infertility Masks

If you're like the majority of those agonizing over the inability to conceive, you spend minutes, hours, days, weeks, and months wearing a mask. Infertility mask = pretending all is well. If you're like me, you wear this mask for years. You let it consume you, and sometimes you even forget it's there. You pretend so you can protect others. You pretend so you can protect yourself. You don't want to be pitied, and you don't want to be assaulted with questions about growing your family. You don't want people to ask if you're okay, and you certainly don't want people to "help." God forbid you get that stupid "just go on vacation comment" one more time. Or, like yesterday, when Aunt Millie suggested you get rip-roaring drunk and have sex, because that worked for her. There isn't a TMI label big enough to cover up that weirdness.

I'm going to offer a lesson so startlingly unfamiliar, you may question my sanity. Deep breaths. Here it goes: *Be Authentic.* Did you implode yet? Take a few more deep breaths, because this is completely opposite to the fake-it-till-you-make-it principle we often hear. What exactly does being authentic mean in this context? It means being completely yourself. It means setting clear boundaries, saying no when you need to, and tolerating other times when you feel well enough to do so. This is about choosing your infertility mask wisely. Wear it when you need to and take it off when it no longer serves you to hide behind it. Everyone is different, of course, so you get to choose your own parameters. I once had a friend and colleague who was also struggling with fertility. She was fully capable of walking into a baby superstore and purchasing items for her friend's shower. She didn't need a mask; she was being authentic. I, on the other hand, would be on the verge of a panic attack. Authentically. In this case, I would take off my infertility mask, refuse to shop for the baby, decline to attend the shower, and send a gift card instead. You might be squarely in the middle of those two scenarios.

Here's the basic idea of choosing to use your mask wisely: When you feel stifled, wound up, tight, tense, or other descriptives that illustrate that crazed infertility-mind thing, it's time to attempt to take the mask off and be your authentic self. When you keep your mask on when feeling horrible, you do nothing toward healing yourself. In fact, you might make things worse (hello, panic attack). For example, you just heard another pregnancy announcement at work and by the time you get home, you're a sobbing mess. When you pick up the mail, you realize your cousin's baby shower invite arrived. Are you going to go? Some people would say "I have to; she's my cousin." No you don't. You always get to choose. If you don't feel particularly stifled, wound up, etc., then perhaps it's okay to don the mask this time and carry on with the thing you don't particularly want to do. The reason to go trumps the reason not to go. If, however, you do feel stifled, wound up, on the verge of a panic attack, etc., then it might be a good time to listen to your authentic self, take off the mask, and say you're not going. Because it's more worth it to protect your spirit and stay home (or do something else to take care of yourself). Nobody, nobody knows more about what you need than you!

Of course, when experiencing infertility, it's quite common to feel wound up and tense at all times, right? So how do you gauge what to do with your mask? For this, I use the "10 Scale." Put the intensity of your emotion on a scale of 1–10. If you're a 5 or higher, it's time for self-care. Consider saying no to whatever is triggering you right then, thereby taking your mask off. No need to pretend all is well. It's so not. In the therapy world, we like to refer to the mask as "boundaries." As you practice this mask thing, you'll become more aware of your individual boundaries. Again, they can be quite different from someone else's—especially your partner's boundaries—and they are constantly moving around. What was once a walk in the park could make you a raving lunatic on another day. That's okay! You're normal. When you get good at noticing and practicing your boundaries, everyone wins. I encourage you to honor yourself and others by regretfully declining their requests. You'll save yourself an embarrassing situation, like a sarcastic outburst at a baby shower that renders people shocked and embarrassed for you. Yep. Been there.

Now, there is one mask that's super useful 100% of the time: the oxygen mask. I'm sure you've heard of the oxygen-mask reference, right? When you're on a plane and the oxygen masks come out of the ceiling due to a change in air pressure, passengers are directed to put their own oxygen mask on first before helping others. This is the mask in the fertility world that's used when you're triggered at an 8 or higher—like the time I got my period at work and a colleague decided to tell me right then that she was pregnant. She had no idea, and I hated to bolt on her, but I had to trade my infertility mask for an oxygen mask, stat!

So, what does the oxygen mask entail? Anything that's radical self-care for you. If you eat chocolate once a year, then radical indulgence or self-care would be to eat one piece of chocolate every day for a week. Get what I mean? For me in the aforementioned instance, it was locking myself in my office, picking up the phone to call my sister, and then leaving early for a mental-health afternoon. I rarely asked for help, and I would just as soon cut off my arm than leave work early. For me, that was radical self-care.

Ultimately, the oxygen mask is what you give yourself in an urgent situation. Perhaps you regretfully decline the baby shower invite and instead go on a mini spa vacation that day. Hey! That's both taking off the infertility mask and owning the heck out of your oxygen mask. You'll totally get an A++++ from me if you do that. And if you're being totally honest, grades motivate you, don't they? I know. I can see you through these pages.

The following exercises are geared to help you home in on this fertility key. Write them in your journal and jot down your answers as they come to you. No need to overthink these; the answers should come as fluidly as if you were taking a sip of refreshing water. Ahhh, authenticity!

Action Steps: Remember Who You Really Are

The truth is simple: We forget who we really are when dealing with infertility, don't we? We get so good at pretending that we ignore how painful daily life is. The following exercises will help you notice when you're pretending and support you in practicing authenticity and self-care.

Exercise 1: Name Your Masks

Name three masks that you routinely use to hide your authentic self from the world. For example, my own mask from the story about my sister I call the "I've Got This" mask. For all anybody knew, I could handle any situation, even though I was breaking inside. Maybe you have an "I've Got This" mask, too. Other masks might include, "I'm Not Scared," "I'm Not Triggered," "I'm Perfectly Happy," "Infertility? What Infertility?" "I'm Not Making Mistakes at Work," "I'm Not Angry," "I'm Not Anxious," and "I Don't Feel Alone." So, tell me: What masks hide the real you? Feel free to write more than three.

1.
2.
3.

Name your top three oxygen masks. That is, what is radical self-care for you? Chocolate? Spa day? Intense exercise? Doing art all day? Feel free to write more than three.

1.
2.
3.

Exercise 2: Ditch a Mask

Okay, here's the true test. Pick one of the masks and commit to ditching it at least once this week (e.g., set some boundaries). How will you do that? Also, pick an oxygen mask that you can commit to using this week. How will you do that? Then do it and write about how it went.

Exercise 3: Journal Exercise

In your journal, answer the following questions:

- Who was I before infertility?
- What part(s) of that person do I miss the most?
- If I could create a new version of myself, even after having experienced infertility, who would I be?
- As a nod to *The One Thing* by Gary Keller, we're going to create a domino effect to you being who you'd like to be. Ready? Here we go. Poof! You are your authentic self from question number three. Really owning that version of yourself, answer the following questions: What are you doing five years from now? What is one thing you can do within the next year to be like that person five years from now? What is one thing you can do in the next month? Week? Today? Now?

Fertility Mantra

Write these words down and put them in a place where you will see and say them (out loud or in your mind) daily. Practice twice a day.

Breathing In: I am authentic.
Breathing Out: I am allowed to say no.
Breathing In: I am authentic.
Breathing Out: I take excellent care of myself.
(Repeat three times.)

Fertility Meditation: Being You

Do this meditation daily for the next ten days. (Reminder: You can access my recordings of this and all other meditations from this book at www.drmariarothenburger.com/transcendingmeditations.)

Being in a comfortable position now, either lying down or sitting up. Begin noticing your breath. Where do you notice it the most? Your shoulders moving up and down? Your belly rising and falling? Maybe it's the coolness of air entering your nostrils and the warmth as the air leaves your body. Simply notice.

Breathing in...breathing out...

Breathing in...breathing out...

And once more, noticing. Breathing in...breathing out.

Noticing your body entirely relax now...beginning from your toes...up to your ankles and calves...thighs and hips...your abdomen and chest. Breathing in and breathing out...watching your shoulders now as they loosen and gently drop.

Releasing all tension you may have accumulated throughout the day or from any tense dreams you may have had. Like a beautiful garden planted in the coral just beneath the surface of the sea, your muscles flow and release with each undulation of breath. Naturally, easily, they let go and experience the waves of your breath.

Watching your facial muscles now, as they release any tension, become heavy with gravity. The muscles behind and around your eyes are letting in more light as they broaden and release any tension held within.

Opening up to the relaxation...your brows are releasing the furrows previously held there...all the tension of your thoughts released into the field. They no longer hold you in their tense prison. The muscles of your scalp relax, and down the other side of your head, the muscles in the back of your neck and down your spine, lower back, buttocks, back of your legs, and down to your feet, bottoms of your feet, and back to your toes. All completely loose, floating, being held by the surface beneath you.

Held in suspension here, as if floating above the surface on which you lie, feeling supported, safe, completely and entirely relaxed.

In this moment, we are going to go on an adventure...an adventure to who you really are. A reminder that you are more than who you seem to be in this physical reality.

Imagine you are standing on a dirt road. What do you see around you? Sky? Trees? Other kinds of vegetation? What do you hear? Animals? Water? Begin moving along this dirt path, noticing each step along the way. Feel the earth beneath your feet, hear the sound each step makes as your feet touch the ground. Feeling peaceful and energized. This state of relaxation is perfectly safe and healthy for you.

Continuing down the path, you notice a fork in the road...take the path that feels most comfortable for you. You are completely safe, and whichever path you choose is the right one. There is no wrong choice.

Continuing down the path you have chosen, you walk until you've come to a clearing. What do you see in this clearing? Perhaps there is more vegetation...flowers? Animals? Walk along farther and notice now a building. It's a house. What does this house look like? Picture it freely now. In as much detail as you can in your mind's eye, imagine the house in front of you.

Standing in front of this home along the dirt road, you now realize you have two suitcases in your hands. They are filled with the grievances of the past. Any pain, any sadness, frustration, anger, solitude, failures, embarrassment, shame, fatigue, and all matter of negative emotion are carried inside these suitcases. Facing the home now, you drop the suitcases in the road. They no longer serve you. You are ready to let them go. Dropping them now. Dropping them onto the dirt road. They are no longer a part of you.

Now, walking toward the house and reaching the front door. There's a sign on the front door that reads the following: "No matter who you are and where you are on life's journey, you are welcome here."

Entering this warm and inviting home now. As you walk into the entryway of this gorgeous home, you notice there is a mirror near the front door. Walk toward this mirror.

Looking into the mirror now. Looking into your own eyes in this mirror, you see your soul there. You see the real you. Everything that is present in our eyes is the real you—not the masks you sometimes feel you have to portray to the world. Looking into your own eyes now, repeat the following: "I completely love and accept you. You are doing the best you can. I completely love and accept you. You are perfect in my eyes. I completely love and accept all of you exactly as you are."

Saying goodbye to your reflection now, you move into a space within the home where you can lie down and relax. Perhaps this is the living room on a beautiful plush sofa. Perhaps you choose a bedroom with an indulgent bed and luxurious linens surrounding you. Perhaps it's outside on a hammock. Wherever you feel most comfortable, head there now.

Feeling like yourself, free of burden, free of self-judgment. Holding compassion for yourself and all you've been through. Breathing in...breathing out...settling into your resting space. You feel the support beneath you, holding you. You are safe. You are secure. You are loved. Faults and all—everything is precisely as it needs to be.

Breathing in...breathing out...

Breathing in...breathing out...

And so it is.

What's Next?

Part of noticing your infertility masks is the awareness that we often do things because we're told we should do them. We should go to school, get good grades, get a good job, etc., right? Goodness, there are so many social norms to wade through, it isn't any wonder our true selves get lost in the mix. Soon, we don't need too much pressure from others; we're hard enough on ourselves! I call this "shoulding" on ourselves. The next chapter expands on the topic of authenticity by addressing the way we beat ourselves up when we feel we aren't doing the right thing or for myriad other reasons.

Chapter Four

Stop Shoulding on Yourself

Forget your perfect offering.
There is a crack in everything.
That's how the light gets in.

– Leonard Cohen

Society is full of shoulds, isn't it? When I was growing up it was "Girls sit demurely. Boys play with trucks. Girls are sensitive. Boys like you if they tease you. You should go to school, get a good job, find a nice boy, get married, have a first (dumpy) apartment, buy a house, be married one year then give birth to your first child, three years later give birth to your second child, work for forty years, then retire."

And while we're at it, in my life, the only right religion was Christianity, one must be heterosexual or go to hell, and even thinking about living with someone outside the confines of marriage was worth a sharp reprimand. As a woman, it was not okay to complain about anything. If I did complain, I was weak and dramatic, a thorn in the side of the unlucky listener of my woes. There is a perfect prescription for us, isn't there? And what if that prescription is not followed to a T?

Failure.

Shame.

Guilt.

Should.

And it's not just society that fills us with shoulds; we should on ourselves all the time. What are the shoulds you say to yourself? "I should have known! I should have done A, so I could have B! I shouldn't have taken the birth control pill for so long! We should've had sex at least every other day during my fertile window! Now this cycle is doomed! I should be a parent right now. I should have provided my parents with a grandchild by now. My spouse should be a parent right now, too. I should go to that baby shower (wedding, anniversary party, kid's first birthday party, etc.)."

What are the shoulds you say to other people? "He should know what I'm thinking! They should know not to say that. She should know what I need right now. My parents should take a hint that I'm not drinking coffee, because I've declined the last three times that I've been here, and they should know that coffee is bad for fertility! My best friend knows all about my conception struggles and should therefore know I'm going to be a bitch when she tells me about her pregnancy."

Think about this: What does it feel like to should on yourself? I mean, you're already down and out from having made a perceived mistake. Then you beat yourself up for it. With my clients, I often have to drive this point home with an analogy. I apologize in advance for this. It's vivid and painful to think about. And it's effective. So here goes: Imagine a sweet little roly-poly puppy happily runs over to you for some love, right? She trips and falls and lands on her back at your feet and wiggles around just waiting for a belly rub. She's all vulnerable and trusting, tongue lolling out the side of her mouth. And instead of bending over to gingerly rub her belly, you kick her.

Yeah. Terrible, isn't it? And guess what. You do that to yourself! You're the puppy! When you make a mistake—perceived or otherwise—you're rolling around on your back looking for some comfort, and then you kick yourself for screwing up. It's not how you would treat that puppy, and it certainly isn't the way to treat yourself. Not if you want optimal fertility, and definitely not if you want to create miracles and a whole new, calmer way of being.

This chapter is all about dropping the shoulds we put on ourselves and others. Stop kicking the puppy! Nobody deserves to be should on, least of all you. Not the friends and family who love you. Shoot, not even strangers on the street. All of us deserve kindness, compassion, understanding, and release from expectations outside of basic humanity. We're all doing the best we can. I'm certainly not exempt from this. The following part of my fertility journey is where I realize my tendency to beat the crap out of myself when I didn't meet my own or others' expectations of me. I'd should on myself so often that shoulding became like my old denim jacket from the '90s (shhh, I stole it from my brother). It had a lot of rips and tears in it, but it was familiar and oh so comfy. Hopefully, shoulding doesn't make a comeback like that denim jacket did.

Here's a not-so-lovely list of some of my shoulds:

- My husband and I should be the perfect couple.
- My husband should know how to handle all my craziness.
- I should be able to get and stay pregnant
- I should not make mistakes. At home, with friends, or at work. Like, ever.
- I should attempt to please people and be 100% selfless at all times, regardless of my own thoughts, opinions, or feelings. In other words, others' thoughts and feelings matter more than mine.

Goodness, that is just the tip of the iceberg. We spend inordinate amounts of time wishing things were precisely how we planned instead of the insanity we experience in trying to grow our family. Because that's how they should be, dammit! Granted, trying to have a baby is not the same as that one time my favorite pair of Nine West shoes were finally worn down and were no longer in stock anywhere. That was a time when things didn't go my way, but I was not traumatized over it. (Well, my husband might beg to differ, but that's beside the point.) Infertility is a wild ride, and I don't know a soul who welcomes it with open arms. We don't need to welcome tragedy with open arms, though; it's more important to acknowledge it, give it a little nod, and when it passes, honor it as part of our process of becoming better versions of ourselves. No shoulds to be had in that process. We can be messy, broken, crazy, and imperfect, and the world will still turn.

The following is the part of the story where our fertility struggles began to rip my shoulds to shreds. I wanted and expected many things to go perfectly;

then infertility showed up like a monster from my closet. It scoffed at my shoulds and took my naivete away forever. Things were not perfect. And they never would be again.

T

T and I met online. That was back when meeting online was not a thing. People asked if I was sure he wasn't an axe murderer. I wasn't. We lived 3,000 miles apart, and we were internet pen pals. Neither of us had ever been pen pals before. I had placed an ad saying I was looking to talk with people who had my same last name. He answered. He didn't have my same last name, but he ignored that part and homed in on the part where I said I wanted to learn to scuba dive. He was certified, so voila! Common interest.

After two years of writing and talking on the phone, we finally met in person. I think I may have decided right then that I was moving to New Jersey, but I'll never tell him that. Shhh. I now call him the world's most perfect grilled cheese: crusty on the outside, and ooey gooey on the inside. Don't be fooled by that sharp tongue and Jersey accent. He's a mush.

Through moving, learning each other's ways, getting engaged, buying a house, and other stressors, T and I were always fantastic. No amount of stress could take us down. Oh, wait. That infertility thing. Yeah, we took a hit there, not going to lie. I've met many couples who claim to feel stronger through infertility. They say their communication is so amazing, they are basically the poster couple for weathering storms. I think that is nothing short of amazing. If there was ever a great test of coupledom, infertility is it. I wish I could say T and I were one of said couples. I wish we opened up and worked through issues, embraced the darkness, and accepted one another's flaws without a second thought. I wish our faces were in neon lights—a literal poster of sorts—our eyes staring adoringly as we touched each other's souls with our gazes. I imagine a caption reading "Infertility couldn't get the best of *this* power couple!" Okay, perhaps that's a bit too much gooey cheese. Even for me.

Still, it would be nice if I could just say we were marginally okay despite our intense struggle toward progeny. I'd be lying if I didn't admit that infertility bitch slapped us. It had us pointing fingers and drove us down the darkest recesses of marital struggle we'd ever known. It started so slowly that, at first, we hardly noticed. We were arguing more and were both coping in our signature ways. He drank more; I ate less. All the while, we ignorantly moved through our sad lives like one of those weird dreams where you're trying to run super fast, yet your legs are caught in some sort of mire and you can only move a millimeter at a time. All the while a lion is gaining on you.

I recall one particularly epic argument when we were invited to T's best friend's house to meet their firstborn son. At this point, we'd failed our first IVF cycle, and depression and anxiety were ruling my life, so I just assumed that T had already declined the invitation. He assumed that I would be dressed, since we were due to leave shortly. After some words back and forth, he yelled, "Is this the way it's going to be for the rest of our lives? We're just going to avoid people and babies and shit?" At the time, I emphatically believed there was nothing wrong with that proposition. I wanted to avoid forever. Or until we had a baby. Maybe even after that. As far as I was concerned, there was no light to be seen in our future, and nobody would ever understand how broken we were. We stopped connecting, stopped engaging, stopped embracing, and stopped being loving toward each other.

Sex was a joke. Depression, anxiety, and not feeling like a "real" woman—due to not being able to conceive—had marred any hope of feeling sensual and attractive to my husband. Of course, forced sessions of okay-I'm-ovulating-let's-get-this-shit-over-with were less than helpful. Have you ever had someone tell you, "Oh, honey, just have fun trying"? Sarcastic laughter is headed their way right now. You're welcome.

Maritally speaking, the lion was upon us. And we were stuck in the mire. We should have been a beautiful couple even under all of this stress. We should have been gentle with ourselves and each other. We should have been able to read each other's minds, make choices selflessly, apologize when necessary, forgive always, and count every single blessing. All those wishes for a perfect partner when I was playing with Barbies as a kid should have been coming true.

Instead, we were a wreck. And at this point, I saw no repair on the horizon. Still, we moved forward on our baby-making track. Following the guidance of the medical community, we pursued IVF number two. It was, after all, what we felt we should be doing. We blindly followed all guidelines for injecting me with the stimulation medication, my ovaries dutifully grew to the size of pomegranates, my body complied by gaining weight and appearing five months pregnant, and we got a few fertilized eggs to show for it. In a daze, I received the news of another Big Fat Negative. And I didn't cry. I felt nothing. Nothing I hadn't felt for the last several years—it was all just one big emotional pain fog. I didn't feel at this point that I could curl up in T's lap while he stroked my hair and told me all was going to be okay, even as he attempted to convince himself of the same. T and I were not okay.

It became apparent to me that our failing marriage couldn't be ignored when we were visiting my father-in-law for Thanksgiving. T's excessive drinking was highlighted as I watched him and his dad twinning out, and I wondered if I could last the rest of my life watching him kill his liver. Coupled with the utter devastation of infertility, I felt entirely alone. Not even my husband was with me, his mind momentarily comforted by the fog of inebriation. Mine was a less comforting fog of depression. Boy, were we a pair.

Like every Thanksgiving for the previous eight years, I called my mom, who was 3,000 miles away. This time I felt that distance like an elephant sitting on my shoulders. I sat on the back patio at my in-laws' home and, after a few pleasantries, let her in on my private hell. I was incredibly unhappy in my marriage, and I wanted out. She cried along with me. It was nice to feel understood.

When we got home that weekend, I told T in my best steady, monotone voice that we were over. I wanted a divorce. He made every desperate attempt to keep us intact, making promises I knew from experience he couldn't keep. Even if I'd trusted him, depression had its claws in my fragile psyche so tightly, I barely recognized myself. The spark was essentially gone from our respective eyes and from this fragile union we'd so fervently promised to uphold on our wedding day.

The days that followed were riddled with grief along with desperate bargaining, anger, and flying accusations. The struggle was our last-ditch effort to salvage even the most minute hope we could discern in the darkness. I recall the day he finally relented. We stood in the foyer of our little starter home after quietly discussing a separation to which he responded, "I don't want to, but if it's going to save us, I'll move out." I replied with unbearable heaviness, "Okay."

And then…silence. It was like the valve formerly allowing all the damage to escape our mouths was shut off, and instantly we were rendered without voice, without reason, and without direction. We hugged and, as if still flailing around slowly in a strange dream, sat on the couch in a daze, pondering our newest decision.

The house was eerily quiet except for the low whirring sound of the fish tank. Our formerly joy-filled home with the incessant laughter and casual romantic gazes was now a cold, uninviting—even unnerving—container of things. No life. No substance. No warmth. Just stuff. All the shoulds I had in my mind were like fingers constantly pointing at me, reminding me how I had failed on so many levels.

T lay on one side of the L-shaped sofa, and I sat on the other. We were simply silent. Spent. It was like sitting at home after a visit to the dentist when your mouth is still numb, but you know the pain is coming. You know it but refuse to acknowledge its impending presence, and you almost enjoy the numbness. I remember staring at him and silently asking myself what life would be like without this beautiful man in my life. It was meant to be a benign question, yet it tore my heart into a billion pieces. That's when the numbness wore off.

Should

If I try to encapsulate the ensuing emotional pain in a handful of words, I'm at a loss. What we stood to lose was monumental; I still cannot quantify it. I didn't care about our things, the house, the furniture, the remodeled kitchen, the newly poured concrete patio. All of it could go. I personally stood to lose his daily laughter, knowing what was going on in his world, what mattered to him. I stood to lose the smell of his clothes and seeing his shoes neatly stacked along the wall as he entered the house. His New Jersey accent that was simultaneously harsh and comforting. The gold flecks in his gorgeous olive eyes accented by the crinkles in the corners when he smiled at me.

Suddenly, our broken, unstable marriage was like shards of gold to me. I was attempting to make my life—our life—look like a picture-perfect world, and I was completely missing the point. I'd had many shoulds spelled out for me. Some even thought T and I shouldn't be together. We were from different parts of the country with wildly different cultures. I was an academic; he worked with his hands. How in the hell did we even match up in the first place? I was beginning to realize in that moment that our individual imperfections made us beautiful. And when our individual imperfections were all gathered up in a display, we were a glorious match. There were no shoulds. We were like art. You know how people say there are rules to art, then an artist comes along and breaks the rules, showing how brilliant art can be? One of my favorite singers, Brandi Carlile, said of her recording of "The Story": "It wasn't technically right, but it felt right." That was T and me. We "shouldn't" have been together, but it felt right.

When I asked myself about life without T as I sat on that couch staring at him, I choked and began to sob. Not even infertility could trump the pain. I recall thinking I would give up having a baby a thousand times rather than lose this wondrous soul. I did not have a solid resolution in play at this point, but there was a spark of something. I knew I was beginning to let go of the shoulds in my life and focus on the things that felt right. I was beginning to be me, and perhaps more importantly, I was beginning to let go of who I thought T should be and appreciate him for exactly who he was.

Infertility be damned, we were going to make it through this.

Fertility Key: Stop Shoulding on Yourself

I had spent a lifetime attempting to achieve perfection. As a kid, I knew my brain would get me far, and I spent a lot of time emphasizing my academic endeavors. Attempting to have the perfect body, perfect life values, perfect sequence of events, marrying at just the right age, having a baby at just the right age—these were all very much in the forefront of my mind. And now here I was. Imperfect.

Not only could I not have a baby, my "perfect" marriage was dissolving before me. At the time, there was not one iota of beauty to be seen. Heartbreak is no joke. Years before I became aware of Brené Brown's work on vulnerability, I was living it daily. And I hated every single moment. I judged myself harshly. I hadn't built up the courage to view the imperfection in my life like a parent would view a child making a mistake, seeing that it's all part of the growing process. Instead, I expected the world of myself, and I wasn't delivering. This is not the way to go. If your goal is to create even more pain, then judge yourself harshly while you're already in pain. But I hope that's not at the top of your color-coded Life Goals checklist.

Instead, I'm making a suggestion: Live a wabi-sabi life. Wabi-sabi is a Japanese principle with wabi meaning "rustic simplicity" or "understated elegance" and sabi meaning "taking pleasure in the imperfect." Note that taking pleasure in the imperfect is more than simply tolerating it; it's actually finding delight in things you might not typically find delightful.

Someone who's living a wabi-sabi life trips and falls in a very public place, begins laughing, then picks herself up, dusts herself off, says, "Well, that was embarrassing," and honors her ability to carry on with her day. She may even have an endearing feeling toward herself for being clumsy or harried in that moment. Like every time a slow driver pulls in front of my car, I know I'm being my typical harried self, and I say to myself, "Okay, Maria—you're being harried again. Isn't that just like you? You love to get shit done. And now here's the Universe telling you (yet again) it's okay to slow down. And it is. P.S. You're valuable and loved even when you're harried."

Believe me when I tell you that ten years ago I couldn't even begin to think about typing that sentence. Now, after all this work and all this practice loving myself, I'm writing with my eyes closed, and it just flows from my fingers, onto this keyboard, and to your eyes. Imagine what your life would be like if you were able to hug your imperfections. Imagine being able to gently shake your head, own your mistakes, and move on. Here's one step further: What if you noticed all the beauty in your imperfections? What if you showed them off to the world, like, "Hey, everyone! Yup, totally screwed up there! Here, I'll highlight it for you in gold!"

I'll tell you what it's like: It's like freedom. It is ease. It is gentleness and peace. It's a solid knowing that you're going to be all right. That your shadow side is fully exposed to the Universe, and that is okay. What about the haters, you ask? What about the ones who will take my vulnerabilities and rip me to shreds? To that I repeat one of my favorite quotes from Brené Brown: "Don't try to win over the haters. You're not a jackass whisperer."

You just get to be you. Let your imperfection shine. Own it like a friggin' boss. Wabi-sabi that shit. If you want to take it one step further, own the haters' imperfections, too. We are all human, after all. Start right now with the action steps below.

Action Steps: Stop Shoulding, Start Cultivating Compassion

We've established the importance of embracing a wabi-sabi lifestyle rather than shoulding on yourself. But how do you close the gap? Cultivating compassion is probably one of the hardest things I had to do during my journey to parenthood. I'd gotten used to kicking my butt into gear and beating myself with each failure (aka kicking the puppy).

The minute I began treating myself with compassion, I felt like a sap, like a weakling, and incredibly undeserving of kindness. It's astonishing how mean we are to ourselves. If someone were walking alongside me and talking the crap that I talked to myself, I'd punch them in the face. If someone were walking alongside me, speaking in full compassion, showing me how to be okay with my imperfect life, and hugging me after I'd made a mistake, I'd hug them right back.

Let's take a look at compassion before we get into the exercises to help promote it. Some folks mistakenly view compassion as pity for another person or oneself. In fact, I've seen some dictionaries define compassion as pity or concern; that is not what I'm talking about here. I like to reference Gregg Braden's beautiful portrayal of compassion. He asks us to think of compassion as the end point in a continuum that looks like this:

Sympathy → Empathy → Compassion

Sympathy is the notion that you can acknowledge someone else's feelings even if you don't have those feelings yourself. For example, I don't know what it's like to be a man, but I can think about what that might feel like. Empathy is the ability to feel another's pain. For example, I've lost a pet before, and I can feel what it's like when I speak with someone who's recently lost a pet.

Compassion is the end of this spectrum. Here's what Gregg Braden says: "Compassion is defined as an emotional experience where we first accept the suffering of another without judgment and without attachment to the outcome—to the rightness or wrongness or goodness or badness. This is what gives compassion so much power. At the same time, we hold the focus for a greater possibility. When we're able to do these things, we're able to transcend judgment." And once we transcend judgment, we're able to move into the realm of possibility. Think about what that means for you. If you're able to accept your suffering as just what it is without assigning a judgment to it (wrong, bad, etc.) and get into the field of possibility, you can begin to create a level of resilience that transcends the woes of infertility, and—poof!—you're braver, more compassionate, more courageous—a better version of yourself than even before infertility took over your life.

> **If you're able to accept your suffering as just what it is without assigning a judgment to it, you can begin to create a level of resilience that transcends the woes of infertility, and—poof!—you're braver, more compassionate, more courageous—a better version of yourself than even before infertility took over your life.**

Got compassion? No? Let's start now.

Cultivating compassion is like any other exercise. You must practice for it to become a habit. It may feel weird in the beginning, like that time I tried ice skating and fell flat on my belly, spinning and gathering more ice as I embarrassingly slid through the crowd of people managing to stay upright. I laughed until my face turned red and eventually got myself back on my skates. Now, twenty years later, I can stay upright on the ice for a whole twenty minutes or more. Standing on ice, balancing on a thin piece of metal without toppling over feels weird in the beginning to be sure, but with practice you come to realize it can be exhilarating.

Exercise 1: Practice Compassion for Yourself

One of the most important things you can do for yourself and your fertility is to offer a sense of peace and ease through self-compassion. I invite you now to write in your journal the following and track it for the next ten days:

Today, on a scale of 1–10 (1 being extremely peaceful), I woke up at a ____ on the scale.

Then, every day for the next ten days, when your eyes flutter open in the morning, do not reach for your phone! If you have to turn the alarm off, fine—but then put that thing right back down. Instead, continue lying down or sitting up in a comfortable position. Then rate your peacefulness on a scale of 1–10, hold your hands on your heart, and say the following to yourself:

May I be peaceful.

May I strong.

May I be flexible.

May I be patient.

May I forgive myself.

May I offer myself complete compassion today.

Then rate your peacefulness again.

Get curious about what you'll see after ten days of practicing this exercise. If after ten days you've become more peaceful and more compassionate, imagine what would happen if you continue doing this simple exercise every day.

Exercise 2: Practice Compassion for Others

You know that thing when the people in your life say hurtful things to you? Perhaps they're trying to be helpful, but they're going about it the wrong way? I gave some examples of these in chapter two; you know, "Just relax and it'll happen"? Sigh. I know how difficult it is to even consider offering up compassion for the folks who say silly, unhelpful things. Yet the benefits of compassion on your body, mind, and soul far outweigh any benefit you get from holding a grudge and envisioning choking the offending party.

Instead, every time you experience an offensive person, consider this exercise on ultimate compassion for them. First, ask yourself, "Did they wake up this morning thinking 'Hmm, now let me see how I can offend [insert your name here] today. Oh I know! I'll say [insert offensive comment here]'?" The likelihood that they woke up thinking about hurting you is very low. If the person you're thinking of would actually wake up thinking about hurting you, then this is an even more important exercise. After answering the above question truthfully, say to yourself (silently or out loud) the following words adapted from Ram Dass:

Just Like Me

Just like me, this person has a body and a mind.

Just like me, this person has feelings, emotions, and thoughts.

Just like me, this person has experienced physical and emotional pain and suffering.

Just like me, this person has at some point been sad, disappointed, angry, or hurt.

Just like me, this person has felt unworthy or inadequate.

Just like me, this person worries and is frightened sometimes.

Just like me, this person has longed for friendship.

Just like me, this person is learning about life.

Just like me, this person wants to be caring and kind to others.

Just like me, this person wants to be content with what life has given.

Just like me, this person wishes to be free from pain and suffering.

Just like me, this person wishes to be safe and healthy.

Just like me, this person wishes to be happy.

Just like me, this person wishes to be loved.

Now, allow some wishes for well-being to arise:

May this person have the strength, resources, and social support to navigate the difficulties in life with ease.

May this person be free from pain and suffering.

May this person be peaceful and happy.

May this person be loved.

Because this person is a fellow human being, just like me.

Fertility Mantra

Practice this mantra in the morning and in the evening for the next ten days.

Breathing in: I am worthy because I exist.

Breathing out: I embrace my mistakes.

Breathing in: No matter what happens in my life

Breathing out: I am whole.

(Repeat three times.)

Fertility Meditation: Practicing Self-Compassion

Do this meditation daily for the next ten days. (Reminder: You can access my recordings of this and all other meditations from this book at www.drmariarothenburger.com/transcendingmeditations.)

Lying or sitting in a comfortable position, look at a point on the opposite surface. Be it a wall, or piece of furniture, or something in nature. Breathing slowly—inhaling, exhaling. Inhaling, exhaling. Fix your gaze on the chosen point across from you.

Begin noticing the lines around that point become more and more fuzzy. Breathing in and breathing out. The lines around the point soon become so fuzzy, you can barely see the point anymore. Noticing how heavy your eyelids are, flutter them closed. Resting, comfortably—all the muscles behind your eyes loosening up, almost a sense of drooping arising.

Noticing now the lines in your forehead and between your brows smoothing out. Relaxing and letting gravity do its job in smoothing out the skin there. On your next out breath, your jaw is completely slack. Watch your jawline fall, and all of your mouth completely relaxed and comfortable.

Breathing in...breathing out...

Noticing now the muscles of your neck and shoulders softening, loosening, letting gravity pull them downward with grace and ease.

The muscles in your stomach, thighs, calves, and feet follow suit. They are completely relaxed, feeling supported by the surface beneath. Notice now the surface beneath you holding you up, supporting you, all points of tension in your body completely released.

I'm going to count down now from 10 to 1. And as I do, noticing you can go even deeper relaxed. Imagine you are standing at the top of a staircase now—the stairs leading to another room. On the edge of the stairs now, stepping down, 10....9....8....

Become deeper relaxed now, knowing this is healthy for you...

7...6...5...

Noticing your breathing becoming deeper, slower, your muscles even deeper relaxed...

4...3...

Very relaxed now—any sounds or sensations outside of you only serve to make you go deeper relaxed...

2...1...

So relaxed now you could not move a limb if you tried. In your mind's eye, imagine looking around the new room you are in. What do you see?

[Long pause]

Now, walking toward the end of the room, you notice a door that leads to the outside. Opening the door now, imagine you are now in an outdoor space. You see a large tree with a swing, and a child swinging with their back to you.

Walking over to the child now, slowly, gracefully, with ease and confidence.

As you come closer to the child, you realize they look oddly familiar. Able to look into the child's face now, you recognize yourself at a younger age.

What age are you?

[Pause]

The you at this age has just made a mistake. What do they feel? What do you want to offer to this younger version of yourself to help with these feelings?

[Pause]

Placing your hands on your heart now, or imagining you are, say those words to yourself now (either out loud or in your mind).

[Pause]

Breathing in…breathing out…

Saying goodbye to this younger self now, knowing you can access them at any time, turn back toward the room with the staircase.

In a moment, I will count up from 1 to 10, as you walk the stairs back up to awake consciousness.

1…2…3…

Slowing walking up the stairs, noticing a little more about the environment around you…

4…5…6…

Breathing in, breathing out. Taking what you've learned about yourself to full consciousness…

7…8…

Moving fingers and toes slowly now…coming back to present

9…10…

Slowly now fluttering your eyelids open. Being here now.

What's Next?

Everything about infertility is about holding on. Holding on to the dream of parenthood, holding on to the notion that the next cycle will result in a live birth, holding on to the idea of catching up with your friends, holding on, holding on, holding on. The problem is, holding on is exactly the opposite of improving fertility, creating miracles, and being a better human. Instead, letting go is the way. Terrifying as that may sound, it's one of the most freeing decisions anyone can make. It's like opening your palm, inviting a little bird to land there, and instead of grasping tightly the little soul that lands there, simply allowing it to stay, without needing it to do anything differently than it's doing.

The next chapter is about cultivating this kind of peaceful existence through the notion of letting go. I know that the idea is terrifying to you; you've held on tightly for so long. I've said it a thousand times: Because you've been through infertility, you've proven you can do hard things. In the grand scheme of things, the letting-go process will feel like a splinter. Okay, maybe fifty splinters, but certainly not the hundreds of IVF needles you may be accustomed to. Take a deep breath. Let's do this letting-go thing.

Chapter Five

Letting Go Is Not Giving Up

DORY: He says it's time to let go! Everything's gonna be all right!
MARLIN: How do you know? How do you know something bad isn't gonna happen?!
DORY: I don't!
— Finding Nemo

A wise and dear friend once said in an interview about her fertility struggles, "Letting go doesn't mean giving up." I immediately loved these words. After all, one of the biggest issues with infertility is that insatiable sensation of lack of control. And unlike other areas of our life where gripping tighter means steering the boat better, when it comes to dealing with infertility, holding on tighter often backfires. It causes a myriad of negative consequences in our bodies, psyches, and spirits, and as we've already explored, this is not good for infertility.

Letting go is one of the biggest lessons to learn while dealing with infertility. It's also one of the hardest because it elicits a trauma response. The act of releasing control of a situation signals the brain's response that we are, well, out of control. The problem is that the brain is coming from a place of trauma when we are actually perfectly safe. Teaching the brain to have a different response to the triggers is no small feat. Why would we want to do this anyway? On the physical plane—or, more specifically, at the level of your body—letting go elicits the parasympathetic nervous system. Think about holding on tightly to something, furrowing your brow, tensing the body in focused concentration. This is all fine and dandy when, say, you're an Olympic athlete or you just need to pass a test in a class. The trouble with infertility is that we hold on tightly 24/7. And the tightening doesn't stop when we resolve our infertility either! Even Olympic athletes know the value of resting, letting go, and recharging. The goal of winning a medal doesn't change, it's just that resting becomes part of the training.

On the level of the spirit, letting go ultimately involves trusting that your desires are on their way to you. They have to be because you put the intention out into the Universe. It is a quantum physical reality that the field knows your intention and is helping create what you seek. (More on the science behind this in a future chapter.) But here's the issue: If the energy you vibrate is about control, holding on tightly, fighting, and all matter of intensity, that's what will come back to you. Notice how this is quite different from someone like the Olympic athlete who holds on tightly, putting in a lot of effort in moments of hardcore training, knowing that what she wants is on its way and that she is creating the action around it. She assumes that the win is on its way. She can feel the win. She is behaving as if the win has already happened. The difference in infertility is that holding on tightly comes from a place of assuming there will be failure. See the difference? That is not what we want to communicate to the Universe. When we let go in mind, body, and spirit while creating through action on the physical plane, we're sending the message that we trust the Universe to listen and create in the field.

The following story is my foray into letting go. I didn't want to; I felt forced to because of circumstances I felt were far more important than making a baby. As you'll read, it wasn't just the dream of growing our family; I let go of many things I'd been latching on to, fearful of letting go and allowing things to be as they were. This part of my story is dark, but I think I needed that darkness to truly let go.

Letting the Light In

The shaking heap on the bed in our tiny bedroom was me. For at least the hundredth time, T and I had had an argument about my insatiable need for a baby. On another anniversary of trying to conceive and still no baby to show for it, I broached the subject of adding another dog to our menagerie of fur babies.

I needed a new baby.
I needed midnight feedings (or potty breaks).
I needed a new little being utterly dependent on me.
We yelled. I cried. He left.

I lay on the bed in the fetal position, sobbing uncontrollably, my mascara staining the pillow cover, as it had countless times over the last eternity—or so it felt. This moment was far more than just the result of an argument with my husband. I lamented all that infertility had taken from me thus far. I no longer knew who I was or where I was going. I no longer felt that T and I were on the same page; sometimes I wondered whether we were even in the same book.

I grieved every single month my period came. With the fresh wound broken open before the whisper of a scab could form, I was raw, exposed, and dying inside. Maintaining my masks was getting harder by the minute.

I went through the motions of my daily activities, pretending to be myself, but Maria was gone. A shadow had taken her place. My soul had somehow escaped my body; in its place: Nothingness. Void. Apathy. Many times I didn't care about finding who I used to be. I vividly recall being stopped at a traffic light thinking about not being alive anymore—what a relief that would be. I drove home over a bridge and frequently wondered what it would be like to drive off it. A faint stirring of fear accompanied those death wishes, yet I received the fear as if from the other side of a soundproof room. I noticed only slightly that I may want to do something about those thoughts, but then I was easily distracted from them.

As I lay there in the heap, thoughts whirling, I felt the bed shimmy slightly. I glanced up to find that my typically boisterous, tail-whacking, underwear-stealing, brownie thief, yellow lab, Bailey had jumped up to be with me. Unusual for him, he refrained from drenching my face in slobber or maneuvering blankets around to make himself comfortable. I wondered what he was doing, but in my darkened state, I was loath to feel entertained. As the sobbing returned, Bailey slowly moved toward me and gingerly, ever so gently, began to lay his eighty-five pounds over my shaking body. And he settled there, allowing me to feel all his weight.

It was as if he meant to say, "It's okay, Mama. I've got this." I was deep in my psychological darkness, and I did not—could not—fully take in the profundity of that moment. Bailey knew I was in excruciating emotional pain—the kind of pain that has no words. The kind of pain that when you look in the mirror and see the distortion living there in the reflection, there is no recognition whatsoever of the person you know yourself to be.

Everything was broken.

But Bailey didn't need words. He didn't need me to look, smell, or talk a certain way. He didn't need anything. He was offering up himself in my time of deep need. And I let him help me.

I let him help me.

I cannot express the stretch it took for me at that time to allow another being to help me, even if it was my dog. You must understand how self-sufficient, controlled, type A, and goal oriented I was. I was the product of an upbringing where the only time you ask for help is when you're dirt poor and can only purchase beans and cereal. And even then, it's shameful. I was taught that one takes care of one's own problems no matter what. To allow someone to take care of me in that moment was a luxury, and I wholeheartedly accepted. I let go of my need to keep my shit together, and let Bailey envelop me. I hardly had the energy to refuse, mind you, but something in me opened up to his gesture of acceptance and love. Bailey knew I needed the warmth, the weight, the unconditional love he brought to me. And even as I write, I think about the truth of the statement "Someday I want to be the kind of person my dog thinks I am."

I didn't know it in this moment, but Bailey would eventually be the impetus for a powerful change in me. Many years since that moment have passed, and I still feel his comforting presence, showing me that if I could let him into my darkness, I could let others in, too.

Four Infertility Years Later...

T and I did eventually get another dog, a miniature dachshund named Dexter. We called him "Monkey," though, because he's constantly jumping and hopping just like a little monkey. To say he was a healing element for me is a total understatement. He was my newest baby, and he knew it. Monkey could do no wrong.

He did not, however, help to mend our broken, infertility-laden marriage. He was a mere distraction. T still drank too much; I still ate too little. I started hanging out with friends instead of going home—anything to be away from a house that was formerly a home enveloped in bright laughter, a place that was a joy for me to return to. Rightfully, we had stopped trying to make a baby, but I still hadn't completely let go of the notion. I was just too exhausted to mend us and my broken lady parts at the same time.

Depressed, anxious, lost, wildly confused, we pressed on. We tried marriage counseling to no avail. If I'm honest, my heart wasn't in it. I didn't trust him. I still loved him very much, but I didn't trust that he would put alcohol far down on the priority list. I also didn't trust myself. I didn't trust that I wouldn't attempt to control him, as any "good" codependent person does. I didn't trust that I wouldn't beat myself up through restricting food if things weren't perfect. But somewhere in there, we knew that pressing on was worth it. So we did just that.

After a few marriage counselors saying, "You guys seem fine!" because we sat on the couch holding hands, we ran into a counselor who helped us make a shift. I don't mean to imply that it was his skill that helped us do so. He asked twice during our session how we intended to pay him. After a few more awkward exchanges, he declared his confusion that we were there in the first place. We seemed to be doing so well (damned infertility masks!). At the end of the fifty minutes, he gave us his card to call in and make our next appointment. T went down the hall to use the restroom, and I headed to the waiting area. The counselor poked his head out of the office and said, "Oh! Did I collect payment?" I reminded him of the check I'd written him seven minutes prior, and we headed out.

As we walked out of the building, I told T what the counselor just said. We made eye contact, noticed the sparkles in each other's gazes, and cracked up. The absurdity of every single part of that counseling session was permeating our fragile world in that moment.

If I were to see that counselor again, I would thank him. Hindsight shows me that it was around that time I realized T and I had a fighting chance. Laughing was rare, but at least it existed. God, that felt good.

Achingly slowly, we began to repair the shreds of our marriage. Gently, honestly, and in the tiniest fractions of our daily lives, we began to move toward healing. Have you ever seen a mountain off at a distance and thought, "Oh! That's pretty close! I bet it's a thirty-minute drive from here," and it ends up being like two hours? That's precisely what healing was like. We'd have a great day, a fine day, and I'd think, "This is going great!" Then the reality would hit, and I'd return to my cave.

Nope. This still isn't safe. I still don't trust him. I still don't trust myself. But I'm still willing. Yup, the willingness is there. Commence dipping toe in. Again.

And that's how it went for an entire year. Back and forth. Ebb and flow. Neither of us knowing whether this was really going to work. But we were willing. We were beginning to let go of the outcome and trust the process. Nothing—nothing—is more powerful than that. We had realized that letting go of control was quite different from giving up.

By the end of 2010, we'd come to a place of solidarity. We were on uncompromised footing, and much more than our toes were dipped into the Pool of Healthy Marriage. We were not 100%, but it was at this time I began recognizing myself in the mirror again, and I knew we were going to make it. This is when I experienced the first miraculous result of infertility: I began letting T be who he was instead of wishing he were different. Yup, he fucked up. So did I. Like, a lot. It was at this point, though, that I began honoring both of our screw-ups and trusted that we were both on our own paths of growth—together. I had no control over his path. And letting go of guiding another person through his shit was like watching an elephant finally stand up after having camped out on my chest for thirty years. Well, shoot, Ms. Elephant! Now that you've stood up, I realized you were there the whole time! Bless you for walking away.

We had also let go of our parenthood journey without giving up. And while our hearts were healing our marriage, completely unbeknownst to us, our son was born halfway across the world.

Fertility Key: Letting Go Is Not Giving Up

I bet the idea of letting go freaks you out.

I bet when you even consider the idea of floating along the choppy waters of infertility rather than desperately swimming for dear life, you momentarily stop breathing. If you are scared out of your mind at the thought of letting go of the process of making a baby, congratulations: You are normal.

I had to learn the whole business of letting go the hard way, and believe me when I tell you I was overwhelmingly resistant to the idea that letting go of the struggle was going to make anything come my way at all, let alone come my way faster. Why shift one's mindset into letting go in the first place? And how is that different from giving up?

Letting Go = Freedom, Trust, Basic belief that all is well

Giving Up = Defeat, Lazy, Resentment

The act of letting go is all about still holding the possibility of your dreams coming true and trusting the Universe to act on your behalf. You sit peacefully, awaiting the manifestation of whatever feelings you put out into the field to be processed. This is super important: Whatever feelings you put out into the field are the feelings that are sent back your way. Letting go is less of an action and more of a mindset or, more accurately, a feeling-set. Get your feelings set on ease, peace, prosperity, a baby—whatever!—and that is what the Universe will put into play for you. Want to feel defeated? Send out those feelings, and that is what will come back to you.

> **The act of letting go is all about still holding the possibility of your dreams coming true and trusting the Universe to act on your behalf.**

And speaking of defeat, giving up is the act of saying "never mind" and not holding on to the possibility of your dreams coming true anymore. There is no trust; there is no ease. There is likely a ton of resentment, bitterness, and anger. Can you see the distinct difference between giving up and letting go?

To help visualize this, consider the following two scenarios:

Giving Up: Sally has been attempting to conceive for two years to no avail. She's been diagnosed with unexplained infertility, and this has made her all the more frustrated. Doctors confirm that she and her partner are healthy, so what the hell is the problem? She's come to a place in her journey where she's angry and bitter, resenting all the pregnancy announcements and baby showers she feels forced to attend. Truth be told, she wants to punch a wall whenever she receives an invitation, but she'd never let anyone know that. She's supposed to behave, be socially appropriate, and smile as if all is well. Meanwhile, she's losing herself, doesn't know what to do next, and blindly follows her doctor's recommendation. She becomes more depressed and anxious as the days continue, while she stubbornly holds on to the notion that she will make this baby thing happen, dammit! After another year of living like this, she gives up. Every day she feels the bitterness and the lack in her life, but at least it's better than the daily struggle of trying to make a baby. She's done trying, even though she continues to feel assaulted by pregnant bellies and cute little families every day.

Letting Go: Sally has been attempting to conceive for two years to no avail. She's been diagnosed with unexplained infertility, and this has made her all the more frustrated. Doctors confirm that she and her partner are healthy, so what the hell is the problem? Even though Sally feels quite perplexed and saddened by her unplanned fertility struggles, she's realized the futility of shoving a square peg into a round hole. She's begun to cultivate peace, ease, and compassion every day while holding the space for her dream of parenthood. In her morning practice, she behaves as if her dream has already come true. As a result, she moves through her day with more grace and peace. She's learned to put her thoughts out into the Universe and let the Universe take it from there. She still feels emotional pain when invited to a baby shower or when she sees a beautiful family at play, but she's able to move through that pain with far less angst than in the past. She's let go of the outcome of her dreams, trusting that all will be well.

This is a an extremely important part: Notice that the letting-go process is not about being completely zen, experiencing no pain, and having the best response at all times. Because that would be im-frigging-possible. It is about being kind to yourself, moving through pain faster by allowing it to exist and trusting that all will eventually be well. Even better way to feel: All *is* well.

> **The letting-go process is not about being completely zen, experiencing no pain, and having the best response at all times. It is about being kind to yourself, moving through pain faster by allowing it to exist and trusting that all will eventually be well. Even better way to feel: All *is* well.**

When I talk about letting go, I'm talking about letting go of both the past and the future. I know you might be saying, "But wait. How am I supposed to manifest my dreams if I don't think about them happening in the future?" Stay with me here because this is incredibly important. When I talk about letting go of the past, I'm talking about past hurts, worries, pitfalls, bad relationships, your mistakes, others' mistakes, etc. When talking about letting go of the future, I mean the need to control the Universe, the thought that the future must go your way. Letting go of the past is pretty obvious, so let's focus on letting go of the future for a moment. There are two parts to letting go of the future:

1. Letting go of the notion that everything you desire must come to fruition exactly how you imagined it.
2. Letting go of the notion that exactly what you desire will come to you in the exact path you imagined it.

There's a subtle difference there, did you catch it? Here's a good representation.

Illustration of Part 1:

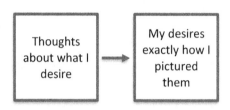

Illustration of Part 2:

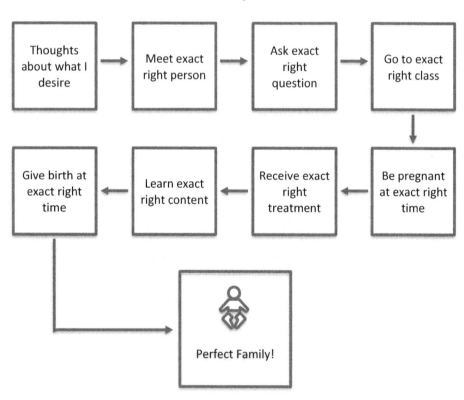

Whew! The first part is hard enough, and then the second part shows up. Geez! You mean I have to get every single one of those parts spot on or my dream is lost? Crazy making, isn't it?

I'm here to tell you, this is a futile effort. Think about an IVF treatment cycle. To follow all the steps involved in a treatment cycle is absolutely mind boggling. Thank goodness clinics create calendars for patients now! And if one part of the cycle is messed up, our brains think we're in the middle of a war zone and panic ensues.

This is the exact way not to practice letting go. It is excessive; it is nerve racking; it is damaging to your body, mind, and soul; and many times it is quite ineffective.

Letting go is superior to holding on at three levels:

At the Level of the Body

Here's where we step away from fight-or-flight mode. You know that saying, "If you love something, set it free; if it's meant to be, it will come back to you"? Imagine grasping your dream, feeling the tension and intensity in your body—the furrowed brow, the clenched jaw, the tight shoulders. Now imagine that the thing you want is hanging out in the palm of your hand. You are not grasping it, desperate to keep it near. When you hold this dream with an open hand, ready to set it free if it wishes, you create more of a sense of ease. You don't force the dream to stay. You let go of intensity, stress, and tension. This takes you out of flight-or-fight mode, engages your parasympathetic nervous system, and increases blood flow to your reproductive organs.

> When you hold this dream with an open hand, ready to set it free if it wishes, you create a sense of ease.

At the Level of the Mind

Letting go is not easy. Or is it? I recall stubbornly resisting the notion that I could let go of something. It felt much better to hold on. This, of course, got me nowhere. If you think about it, efforts to desperately hold on are born out of fear. When we act out of fear, it's like giving the fear a piece of candy. It's only going to want more. So you have to continually assuage it. "Okay, Fear, here's another piece of candy; I'll do whatever you want." Instead, when you use your frontal lobe—your clear thinking—you remember that you are the boss of your mind. You get to tell your brain what chemicals to emit. And the more you tell your brain how to respond to fear, the less you're giving it candy. When you continually remind yourself that you're safe—and begin living as if all is well and safe, rather than from the horrors of the past when things did not feel safe—you begin to consciously create your future.

At the Level of the Spirit

This is my favorite part. It's where shit gets real. Yes, mind and body may seem more real to you, but nothing can exalt the realm of possibility like Spirit can. Let me offer some clarity on that last statement. (I'm about to get nerdy, so hang in there with me.) There is real scientific evidence supporting the theory that the universe is all One. Everything is connected, and there is an invisible field all around us where we send and receive information. You know that thing when you go to call someone, and then they send you a random text? Weird, right? And it's not random. You sent them information through the field, they thought of you, and they texted you. Voila! Seeming coincidence. Now, you may be asking, "Hey, Maria, why are you talking about science when this is a section about Spirit?" Well, I'm happy to say that the gap between science and spirituality is being closed. We're getting closer every day to realizing that the spirit realm exists and that we humans are more powerful than we thought possible. I don't care if you want to call it God, Yahweh, Universe, or Lollipop, the energy is there for your use.

Now, this is the most exciting part about Spirit and the letting-go process: When you let go of the way things "should" be, you become open to the realm of possibility. You become open to the realm of the way things could be if you lean into the idea that things do not need to be precisely as you imagined. First you imagine the feeling of what you want, then you let go of the outcome. Eventually, the feelings you desire are made manifest through something concrete. It might look like this:

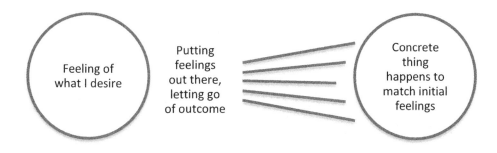

Note: the concrete thing could look nothing like what you imagined. But it doesn't matter! Because you feel the feelings you initially put out there.

There's some more action before the concrete thing happens, though, and that brings me to the next part of having all you desire. The next step in the letting-go process is a series of choosing your next move based on what your intuition is telling you, constantly keeping your initial feeling goal at the forefront. Your intuition will match your feeling goal to your next move incredibly well. That process looks like this:

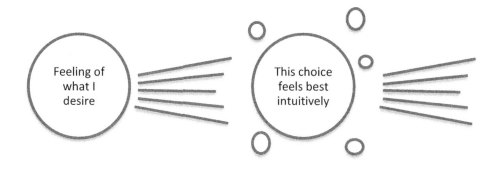

(Repeat until concrete thing is made manifest)

In a future chapter, we'll talk in greater depth about accessing your intuition. For now, know that letting go actually puts you in more control than you've ever had regarding your fertility journey. Moreover, you'll be in more control with less effort, more ease, more peace, more tranquility, and more solid belief than you've yet experienced. Now who wouldn't want that?

The next section will help you get started in the letting-go process. Lean into the discomfort here. It may not be easy, but it's worth it.

Action Steps: Staying Present, Letting Go, Surrendering

If you're not ready to directly practice letting go of your struggles, make it your practice to stay present until you are ready to begin letting go. Don't force the practice; anything that encourages forcing, fighting, or battling engages the sympathetic nervous system, which we've already determined is something to be immediately avoided. Instead, practice staying present. One need only conduct a quick internet search on mindfulness practices to get a plethora of ideas (be careful not to go down the Dr. Google rabbit hole, though).

At the very least, once per day, pause in your hustle, bustle, and attempts at multitasking and simply *be*. Set an alarm on your phone as a reminder to sit in the middle of the room and just drink a cup of tea. That's it. After a few times doing this, you'll notice there's quite a lot to pay attention to. Sometimes when I'm enjoying my favorite Bengal Spice tea during quiet moments, I'm able to pick out individual spices and even feel the texture of the tea on my tongue. Eventually you'll begin to crave these moments of tranquility. Once you do, you will have reached the point where letting go and surrendering to the moment becomes second nature. You can use this skill in harried moments, traffic jams, and surprise pregnancy announcements.

One of the biggest things I hear from people who are just starting to practice mindfulness is "I can't meditate. I just keep having thought after thought, and then I just get frustrated and quit." Want to know my reply? The fact that you're noticing you're having thought after thought *is* the practice. Say what? Yes! Noticing you are thinking, noticing you are breathing, noticing the birds outside, noticing your dog snoring on the bed next to you—whatever you are noticing in the present moment is the practice of mindfulness. The frustration comes when we judge ourselves—when we should on ourselves (see chapter four for a refresher on this). Let me tell you, I get it. I remember how annoyed I was that I was not able to sit for long with a small smile on my face like the many Buddha statues I'd seen over the years. "Screw that," I thought. "I'm just not a meditator." I didn't realize that the act of noticing was all it took to be a meditator. Once I heard this from a meditation teacher, I was able to begin to practice moving on neutrally whenever I noticed my thoughts rather than silently berating myself.

My favorite thing to say to newbies is, "Meditation don't care!" Meaning, if meditation were a person, it would be right there waiting when you're ready to attend to it again. Even if your mind wanders a hundred times in a five-minute session, meditation will still be waiting with open arms, ready to offer its warm embrace and joyful smile whenever you're ready again. And if you're not ready to attend to it again, it will still be waiting with open arms, ready to offer its warm embrace and joyful smile.

Exercise 1: "5, 4, 3, 2, 1"

Here's one of my favorite grounding exercises that is simple and rooted in staying present. When finding your thoughts taking you anywhere but the present moment, simply complete the following directives.

Take a deep breath.

Name 5 things you can see.

Name 4 things you can hear.

Name 3 things you can touch.

Name 2 things you can smell.

Name 1 thing you can taste.

Take a deep breath.

Exercise 2: Create a "Letting-Go Box"

If you're particularly crafty, you're going to love this exercise. I want you to create a "Letting-Go Box." You could also call it a "Give-It-to-God Box," "Jesus-Take-the-Wheel Box," "Leave-Me-Alone Box," or anything else that resonates with you and means letting things go. I once saw a t-shirt with a silhouette of the Buddha with a caption that read "Let That Shit Go." A) I need that t-shirt and B) what a fantastic idea for a Letting-Go Box! Just saying.

The box can be made of anything: wood, a shoebox, styrofoam, cardboard, whatever you have on hand. You'll want to make a mail slot at the top to drop notes into. Whenever you have a worry, fear, frustration, sadness, or any other negative thing you wish to release, you'll write it down and drop it into your Letting-Go Box. I personally like the flourish of dusting my hands off after dropping a worry into the box, but that's optional. One major thing I like about this letting-go process is the attitude with which a worry is let go. There's no disdain, no conquering, no war, no fight—it is simply the energy of letting go. If we take it one step further, you'll notice that you've made a lovely box in which to give away your worries. That means these worries are precious. They are part of you, and historically, they have meant to keep you safe. When you honor them in this letting-go process, you lovingly say, "Thank you for trying to keep me safe all this time; it no longer serves me to hold on to you. You can go now. Thank you." Boom! Your parasympathetic nervous system kicks on, your health improves, your spirit is lifted, and you've completed a great practice in letting go.

If you are not particularly crafty and/or don't want to make a box, simply create a page in your journal specifically for your letting-go practice. Jot all your thoughts there, close the journal, and set it aside. Each time a new worry comes up, practice letting it go in this way. There's still a physical practice here of letting the thought go, and you'll notice immediate relief.

Fertility Mantra

Practice this mantra in the morning and in the evening for the next ten days. Feel free to substitute the word "worry" for any other negative thought you may have.

Breathing In: Worries have kept me safe in the past.

Breathing Out: Worries no longer serve me.

Breathing In: I honor worry.

Breathing Out: I lovingly let worry go.

(Repeat three times.)

Fertility Meditation: Body Scan

The following meditation is the most challenging exercise I completed during my fertility journey, and I wouldn't be surprised if it is for you, too. It's profoundly simple, yet the meaning behind it and the realizations I had during it were inordinately eye opening. This is a simple body scan, which means noticing different parts of the body. In the exercise below, I ask you to systematically tighten parts of your body and then practice letting go by releasing the tension. This was difficult for me on two levels: 1) With every ounce of my being, I was terrified of letting go, and 2) I hated my body and did not want to notice anything about it, especially because I was hyperaware of every fertility and pregnancy sign.

If you struggle with similar difficulties, you're completely normal. This exercise is designed to help you practice letting go very safely. Be in a familiar space when you do this and surround yourself with things you love. It's essential to feel safe while letting go.

The second difficulty is the harder of the two. Sometimes people can get quite triggered by noticing the nuances of the body after having gone through infertility (or other traumas). If you have an adverse reaction to this exercise that takes you to an 8 or more on a scale of 1–10 (10 being panic), stop the exercise immediately and practice Exercise One in this chapter instead. You'll need to re-ground yourself. On the other hand, if you're at a 7 or below, you're giving your brain a healthy dose of education on how to handle stress, even though it may be uncomfortable. You're growing new synaptic connections that tell your body, "Even in the midst of a trauma trigger, I can stay safe, I can move toward calm, I can move toward peaceful." Trust yourself and practice feeling your own limits.

Do the following meditation for the next ten days. (Reminder: You can access my recordings of this and all other meditations from this book at www.drmariarothenburger.com/transcendingmeditations.)

With your eyes closed, lying down on a supportive surface, take three slow and deep breaths. Letting your feet fall to the sides, your arms are beside you or in another comfortable position. Notice the surface beneath you, the temperature of the air, and begin noticing your body respond to your breath. Your stomach and perhaps your chest rise and fall. Simply notice.

Imagine you can breathe in a beautiful energy around you. You may consider giving it a color, any color you choose. And each time you inhale, the light follows. Imagine also that you can exhale toxins or negative energies. Give them a color as well. Each time you exhale, notice that color leaving your body.

Inhale…

Exhale…

Inhale…

Exhale…

We are going to complete a progressive body scan beginning with your toes and finishing with your head and face. This practice involves intentionally tightening up various parts of your body and letting them go. It's a practice in physically letting go of tension, so you can move forward with letting go of mental and emotional tension.

Each time you are directed to let go of tension, you may notice a slight resistance to doing so. This is normal. Notice the resistance and practice letting go anyway. This practice is safe. You are safe. And the letting go process is very healthy for you.

Notice now, your toes, feet, and ankles. What do you notice there? A temperature? A tingling sensation? Tension? Nothing?

Now, squeeze your toes and feet as hard as you can for five seconds, then release.

5, 4, 3, 2, 1.

Notice what it is like to feel the release of tension in your toes. Is there a change from what you noticed before? What was it like to release the tension? Was there resistance? Pleasure? Relief? No change? Simply notice.

Moving up now to your shins and calves. We are going to repeat the process. Tighten those muscles now as hard as you can without too much discomfort for five seconds.

5, 4, 3, 2, 1.

And release. Again, notice the release of tension. No judgment. Simply notice.

Now it's time to focus on your thighs and hamstrings. As before, tense up these muscles tightly for

5, 4, 3, 2, 1.

And release. Notice the changes happening.

On to your hips and buttocks. Tighten for

5, 4, 3, 2, 1.

And release. Notice. Simply notice.

And your belly and lower back now. Tighten these muscles now for

5, 4, 3, 2, 1.

Releasing them gently now. Noticing the release. Just noticing.

Moving up to your solar plexus, chest, arms, and hands. Tighten all of these areas as much as you can for

5, 4, 3, 2, 1.

Releasing now. Noticing any sensations in these muscles.

Up to your shoulders, upper back, and neck now. Many people carry extraordinary tension in these muscles; it may feel especially good to let this area go. Tighten now for

5, 4, 3, 2, 1.

And release. Letting all of the worry, fear, tightness, and negative energies leave this area of your body. No more holding on; just letting go. And notice the release.

Lastly, your face. There is an intricate system of muscles in your face; many muscles to tense up. Let's do so now. Tighten for

5, 4, 3, 2, 1.

Releasing the tension now. Noticing your bottom jaw move gently away from your top jaw. Noticing the grooves move out of your forehead. Perhaps you notice your eyes spreading farther apart from one another, the muscles behind your eyes completely dissolving into calm bliss. You may even notice your ears dropping slightly. Are there any sensations on your scalp?

Breathing deeply again now three times.

Inhaling light, wellness, a sense of ease...

Exhaling tension, worry, stress...

Inhale...

Exhale...

Inhale...

Exhale...

And when you're ready, slowly moving your fingers and toes, fluttering your eyes open, and carrying on with this peaceful day or preparing for your evening.

What's Next?

Have you ever been in a fog? I mean a literal fog. I was recently in a fog on my way to work as I crossed the pedestrian bridge to our lovely downtown. Typically, the scene I find there is spectacular with the metal and concrete of the bridge contrasting with the majesty of nature all around. It's autumn as I write this, and the bold hues of yellow, orange, and red reflect gorgeously in the river below me as I make my daily commute. The day that I'm speaking of, though, none of the beauty was evident, as a cold fog had settled into the valley, and everything beyond the bridge was covered in milky white. I could hear the river below, and I could hear the trees moving in the breeze, but I couldn't see anything except the metal and concrete of the bridge and the homes of spiders who likely found much to feast on there above a river.

I knew that the river, trees, fish, and birds were somewhere there in the fog, but I couldn't see them. When the fog lifted at the end of the day, during my afternoon commute back home, there they were again, waiting to be seen.

Once you've begun practicing letting go, a wondrous thing happens: You begin to notice the other parts of your life that were there, shrouded under the fog of infertility. You may begin to realize you've missed parts of yourself, and you've missed out on many aspects of life. The next chapter encompasses putting infertility in its rightful place, so you can begin living a well-balanced life. Like the nature around me on the bridge, there are parts of you waiting to be seen again when the fog clears.

Chapter Six

Shrink IF

If you ever find yourself in the wrong story, leave.
—Mo Willems

During your infertility journey, have you ever had the realization that you aren't yourself anymore? Have you ever resented not doing the things you used to do for fear of thwarting your efforts to create a family? What about that vacation you wanted to go on? Did you cancel it because it may have fallen during your IVF cycle? Or perhaps you would be pregnant, therefore bedridden? Did you stop exercising or drinking your favorite morning latte because somebody told you both were bad for fertility? What about your favorite hobbies? Gone? Do you catch yourself watching someone walking by you and wondering whether they're pregnant even though they aren't showing?

When we struggle with infertility, everything becomes about it. No decisions are made without first consulting our inner fertility calendar and what might be happening at the time we may want to plan something. Suddenly we find ourselves reclusive, resenting infertility, and not fully living our lives. For me, infertility became everything. I had lost who I was. My whole identity was wrapped up in making a baby. Sound familiar? I was no longer a therapist, wife, fur-mama, gardener, reader, wannabe pianist, optimist—and a whole host of things. Suddenly I was an Infertile. The end. Oh, wait. Pessimistic Infertile. Yeah, that's more like it.

> When we struggle with infertility, everything becomes about it. Shrinking IF is about making infertility important, but not everything.

I'd noticed many times how quickly life was passing me by; however, it was all within the context of people having babies. "Well, they're now pregnant with number two, and they started trying for the first after us!" My heart hurt every time I noticed people moving on. I felt stuck. And I made that stuck feeling my whole life. We forget that making a baby is just one part of our whole lives. We are so much more! And if we get bogged down in one aspect of our life, the rest of it will simply move on.

This chapter highlights the need to put infertility back in its rightful place in your life. Shrinking IF is about making infertility important, but not everything. Imagine if you could simply plan and go on a vacation with nary a worry about an impending cycle. Imagine if you could say yes to being a maid of honor and not worry about whether you'll be able to drink at the wedding. Imagine not worrying incessantly about attending family events and having to dodge family-building questions. Imagine that infertility is important and not at the center of your universe. It took a wake-up call in the form of tragedy for me to put infertility in its rightful place. I hope that's not what it takes for you. Yet the role of infertility is so powerful, I understand if that's what it takes. May the following story help propel you toward making infertility a smaller part of this glorious life's journey.

Bailey

"He's in exquisite pain," the vet said. Bailey had only a small percentage of his kidneys left, due to a disease he hadn't shown any signs of until a few months prior when he would do these odd stretches after intense exercise.

T and I were emerging from an incredibly dark place. Infertility had zapped us of our strength and vitality, and we were floating our way up out of the despair. I was still quite depressed and anxious, but I was learning to take care of myself a bit better and trust that T was also taking care of himself. I questioned the wisdom of the Universe at throwing a giant wrench in the works on top of our still-fragile marriage. What. The. Frig.

As Bailey writhed on the sterile floor of the emergency vet's office, I stood frozen in utter shock and eventually walked mummy-like through the process of getting him the care he needed.

The next two weeks were a blur. In and out of vet offices, intravenous fluid, seeing my precious pup in pain and confusion. If you're an animal person without human kids, you know what I mean by your animals being your kids. And the insatiable need to have them feel better, see the sparkle return to their eyes, and feel their slobber on your face is all-encompassing. After two weeks of treatment, however, the vet gave us the unavoidable news that Bailey wasn't getting better. And if he did, the condition of his kidneys would render his quality of life barely a shadow of his vivacious self. We could not allow that. I'll never forget the look in his eyes the last day at the vet's when he got up to walk toward me despite being in agony. Dogs don't talk, but they communicate especially well. "Just take me home, Mama. Take me home."

We stopped treatment and took our boy home to live his last few days. A gracious vet came to our home to bring Bailey to peace. He lay in T's lap while the vet fed our precious son the poison that would be his freedom from a failing body. Except for the sound of disbelief and raw emotion, there was utter silence in our house that day. Even our yappy dachshund intuited the gravity of that hour and stayed close by his big brother.

The vet and her assistant excused themselves while we said goodbye.

T looked at me in anguish. "I just felt his last heartbeat," he managed to sob out. We sat rocking our boy and saying goodbye to his precious soul while the peace gently entered the room. And just like that day when Bailey's body covered mine in my emotional pain, T's body covered Bailey's as he left it.

Once again, tragedy enveloped us in its wisdom and moved us toward a strength we had not known until that moment. In my intense grief, I wrote our precious boy a letter to help process through it all.

Dear Bailey,

I remember well that day we got the phone call from our friends saying they had buyer's remorse and do we know anybody who would want a puppy. You were ornery from the start. Dada looked at me and said, "You wanna go see him?" I knew right then: You were going to be ours.

Our friend barely had a chance to open his apartment door before you came waddling through to greet us. You were a roly poly little thing at 8 pounds and 8 weeks old, and you wanted to be friends with us immediately. We wanted to take you home and shower you with love immediately. The three of us were a perfect match.

In no time you were being ornery at our house instead of our friend's. You chewed shoes and shredded books and pulled on your leash when we weren't walking fast enough (which was basically 100% of the time). You jumped on us and bruised our legs with your strong, lashing, happy tail. You stole socks from the hamper and underwear from the bathroom floor, all the while giving yourself away with that eye twinkle that always told on you.

Remember the first time you swam in the lake? I was a nervous, nervous mama, completely forgetting that it's what you were bred to do. Dada threw your bone way, way out in the lake. You happily dove in and swam, swam, swam until you reached it, never seeming to tire. You couldn't wait to bring it back so Dada could throw it out again…this time even farther! Do you remember me giggling like crazy seeing you swim all that way as little as you were? We always joked that you would swim until you died; It was your favorite thing. Next to cookies and cuddles.

Actually, you have a huge list of favorite things. Let's start with those three:

- Swimming
- Eating cookies
- Cuddling
- Playing "stick"
- Running in the park
- Meeting new people
- Popping new basketballs/soccer balls
- Chasing squirrels
- Hiking
- Sniffing new and amazing things
- Eating tomatoes from Mama's garden
- Eating gum from Mama's purse
- Stealing stuff from the counter (oooooh…this should be highlighted).

- Getting belly rubs
- Playing with your "squeaky boy" toy.
- Hearing Mama sing your silly song and watch her do your silly dance
- Falling asleep at the foot of the bed (crowding Mama in the process)
- Waking up and spending time with just you and Dada in the morning
- Showing Dada and Mama your fancy tricks (followed by cookies, of course)
- Watching Mama cook

I could go on and on forever, my precious boy. You know why? Every moment of every day was spectacular to you. It didn't matter what you were doing, you enjoyed it. You brightened our every day with your antics and silliness, and you let us know that we brightened your days, too. Too many kisses and cuddles from Bailey is impossible.

There are many things that we wish we did differently. We blame ourselves that we are losing you so soon and so suddenly. We didn't have enough time with you! Of course, there is absolutely no way that we could express in even a thousand years how much we love your spirit. So, even if you lived to a decrepit age, we still would've felt that we didn't have enough time with your beautiful soul.

I'm convinced the Universe gave us just the right amount of time we needed with you to get a taste of what Heaven is like.

One of my friends recently reminded me that our bond with you is eternal. You know what that means, handsome boy? It means that when we meet again, you'd better be ready for a serious game of "stick" and a swim in the lake…forever.

We know you'll be waiting for us.

With inordinate Love and Light to you, Puppa Deeda, we say goodbye for now, but not forever.

XOXOXOXOXOXOX,
Dada & Mama

P.S. Give Grandpa and Uncle Andy one of your tail love-whacks for me, will ya? And don't forget Oma and Opa and Grandma Carol.

P.P.S. Don't wait too long before you visit us in our dreams.

That Spring...

I sat on the patio, the concrete warming my behind, the sun warming my face. The lavender I'd planted three years earlier was full and fragrant, swarming with bees. This was one of my favorite spots in the backyard. It used to bring such peace.

Today, though, my despondency robbed me of the usual pleasure I had at inhaling the warmth of lavender and sitting alone in my space. Come to think of it, despondency had been ruling my life for five and a half years—ever since infertility decided to take over.

This moment among the lavender was about to change everything. This is the moment I began to shift into a heightened level of clarity. Once again, I began letting go, but this was more than the passive shift I'd experienced while repairing a broken marriage. This time, it was a decision. Sometimes the profound things hit you when you least expect them.

Over in the corner, near the shed, was a stick about a foot and a half long, leaning against the building. It seemed like an arbitrary stick and seemed to have haphazardly landed after having fallen from a nearby tree.

But this was no ordinary stick.

This was Bailey's stick.

Whether we threw a ball or a stick, Bailey ran ceaselessly to retrieve it and bring it back, his tongue lolling out the side of his mouth, splashing spittle in every direction, and his monster tail wagging so hard his behind would follow suit.

When my eyes fell on the stick, I realized that I'd never throw it for Bailey again. And my heart sank. At that time, I was moping around the house in grief, expecting to see him turn the corner and follow me around, as was his custom. I lay in bed once and felt the foot of the bed move; I looked up reflexively to see my sweet boy curled up there, but alas, he was not.

Sitting on the patio and looking at his stick, I realized that infertility had robbed me of a lot of precious time with Bailey. Rather, I had let infertility take over.

W. T. F.

I was so caught up in my life of trying to make a baby, that I did not live my life. Bailey lived his life every single minute. I did not. My marriage had barely begun surviving again, my precious fur baby had not survived, I did not feel the same passion for work that I used to, I was depressed and anxious, and I didn't do anything for fun anymore. I couldn't! There was no time for that! I had to go to appointments, obsess, do my internet searches, try anything to make a baby. I didn't have time to be in the moment with Bailey or anybody else.

In short, I had given my life to infertility.

> **I was so caught up in my life of trying to make a baby, that I didn't live my life. I didn't do anything for fun anymore. I couldn't! There was no time for that! I had to go to appointments, obsess, do my internet searches, try anything to make a baby. In short, I had given my life to infertility.**

Bailey's death was a serious wake-up call about what my life had become. No. More.

Infertility could suck it! And I, Maria T. Rothenburger, was getting my life back, dammit!

I would not miss valuable time anymore. I would not stop making plans for fun with T. I would not stop planning vacations. I would not be a social recluse anymore. I decided I would not give one more solitary second over to infertility. Rather, I was choosing life.

And oh, the freedom of that choice! Just writing about it now, I feel like dancing! I once met someone who randomly began painting one day, and they were stunning paintings of horses. She exclaimed, "I didn't even know I could do that!" The freedom of this choice was like that—like discovering a talent you didn't know you had.

I need to be abundantly clear: Making this decision didn't mean I didn't want to be a parent anymore. It meant I was cool with how life was in that moment. I'd become well practiced in letting my dream of parenthood go so that it could willingly find its way back to me. And I trusted that it would. I began finding joy in ways that I would not have if I hadn't experienced this shift. I began gardening, doing projects around the house, making music, savoring food, making art, and hanging out with people who mattered to me. I began noticing everything that was beautiful around me. I would watch the movements of birds in my yard or even little bugs, wondering what they were after. I documented the sowing and harvesting of my garden and thought, "Holy crap! I can grow things!" It brought me such joy to be able to take vegetables and fruits to the office for others to enjoy. But more than that, I noticed the minutiae of the fruits and vegetables—their shapes, colors, fragrances. Everything about them was a miracle to me.

My light was coming back.

And as my light came back, the world seemed different. It wasn't better. And it certainly wasn't worse. There was a peace infiltrating my experience that reminded me of the day Bailey left this world. It wasn't that I didn't feel pain; it was that I honored the pain, and I honored the possibility of movement toward tranquility and joy I had not known before.

I still thank Bailey for prompting this divine shift in my consciousness and for teaching me the profound notion that I could let go of my fears while remaining steadfast in my dreams. And most importantly, he taught me to live. Live. Right. Now.

Fertility Key: Shrink IF

As I was learning to enjoy my life again, I realized that the infiltrating essence of infertility had diminished. Similar to the process of letting go, I didn't realize how absolutely uptight and controlled I was in making infertility everything. All decision-making in my life had to do with where I was in a given cycle, and I certainly couldn't make any big plans, because I could be pregnant and wouldn't be able to travel.

When I started actually living again, I realized the freedom inherent in shrinking the importance of infertility. I began to play the piano again, write, create, grow things, crochet, and read just for friggin' fun! I was getting *me* back again! I wrote this blog post after our first failed IVF about missing who I used to be:

> I was sitting here thinking the other day (slowly becoming one of my least favorite habits), and I noticed that my thoughts have just been so freakin' negative lately.
>
> That's NOT me!
>
> In my former life as an optimist, I was always bright eyed, happy, and willing to push through to the next step. In my present life (but not permanent life), I am angry, negative, and just plain tired.
>
> For the past four days, I have done next to NO exercise, I've eaten junk, I've cried, I've sobbed, I've screamed, I've hit things, I've hugged and kissed the crap outta my hubby and animals, I've scowled, I've found delight in next to nothing, and I've just been a complete bitch to be around.
>
> I forgive myself.
>
> I subscribe to a magazine called *Body & Soul* (I SO recommend it). I know…seems like a random thought. But there was an article in there that talked about recovering from a traumatic event, which of course is exactly what I'm doing. It talked about finding things to be grateful for. All my training tells me that is exactly what I need to be doing, yet there's this stubborn resistance ebbing and flowing in me. I've decided that I miss me…the old me.
>
> So, I'm going to push through this stubborn resistance and find something to be grateful for every day. I'm keeping a notebook in my purse and writing it down. Starting now.
>
> Grateful thing #1: My husband. The day we found out about our BFN he was incredible. Pushing through his own grief, he comforted me like a champ. He wouldn't leave my side. He cried along with me. He wiped my tears. He rubbed my back. He said, "We're going to get through this." He said, "It's all going to be okay." He bought me hummus. Short story: He HATES when I eat hummus (garlic breath). If I were in better spirits, I would have laughed out loud. I have looked at him daily since then and wondered what I would have done without him. I literally have no idea. He is amazing. He is my rock. And I am so grateful that he is who he is.

It's easy to look back at this story and see how I began to be myself again. It's easy to note that the cheerfulness, the openness to experience, and the delight in the little things were returning.

But there was so much more.

I bore the scars of a trauma I wouldn't wish on my worst enemy. And I smiled while bearing those scars. I was still fragile, but I was taking care of myself and telling infertility that it was no longer the be-all and end-all of my existence. I was on my way to ultimate strength and ownership of my pain, healing, and scars. I knew I was going to be okay because I was practicing gratitude, loving life precisely how it was, and honoring those moments when I felt broken all over again.

Nowhere have I seen this concept portrayed as beautifully as I have with the Japanese pottery technique called *kintsugi*. I once saw this artistry displayed on a morning news show and was transfixed by the beauty before me on the screen. Fully embracing the wabi-sabi way of life, kintsugi potters see broken bits of pottery in their artist minds as a way to propel the particular piece forward to another—perhaps better—version of itself. Kintsugi pieces are carefully pieced back together for display or use again, but the fact that these pieces are gingerly and reverently held back together is not the best part. Kintsugi potters highlight the cracks of the broken pottery with gold. In effect, the pottery tells a story of its creation, its struggles, and its ability to carry on despite the scars now advertised quite openly. It's as if the pieces cry out, "Yup! I was broken. And the brokenness invited in the precious, precious gold and accentuates all of who I am."

This process mirrored the changes in me as I ventured this new path of living life and curbing infertility. I felt beautiful in my growth. Infertility had fundamentally changed me in that I no longer harbored a secret plan to control the universe, and I could appreciate all the new experiences that came my way. I was able to see the indelible scars that infertility had left on my psyche, and I was able to notice how the scars had helped me transform into a human with far greater depth and understanding of humanity than I'd previously thought possible.

> Kintsugi potters highlight the cracks of the broken pottery with gold. In effect, the pottery tells a story of its creation, its struggles, and its ability to carry on despite the scars now advertised quite openly. This process mirrored the changes in me as I ventured this new path of living life and curbing infertility.

Infertility wasn't on the outside; nobody could see it. Nobody could see that I was breaking, dying, and cracked inside. Outwardly, I was awful to people—judgy, pushy, irritable. This was all due to my inner pain. And, of course, I kicked myself every chance I got.

What if other awful, judgmental, pushy, and irritable people were also experiencing inner pain that they could not properly express? What if they feared highlighting their brokenness too?

Shrinking infertility allowed me to see the possibility that I was not alone, that others hurt too, and that I was perfectly capable of offering compassion to all of us. More than that—like the artists who highlight the cracks of the broken pottery, I knew intuitively that the more I was able to highlight my own cracks, the more beauty I would find and, therefore, be able to see in others. It's also important to note that the cracks weren't everything. Yes, the cracks are messy, imperfect, and beautiful. But they wouldn't exist without the unbroken parts. This is what it means to shrink infertility. This is what it is to shrink the power that infertility holds over you. Yes, infertility is important. But it isn't everything.

When you're able to see every part of yourself—your delight, brokenness, intelligence, beauty, strengths, weaknesses, anxiety, confidence, and abilities—you begin to transcend the limits of infertility-mind. You begin to realize you are vastly more than even your physical body can convey. Your consciousness, your Greater Self, the part of you that is all knowing, is an intelligence unmarred by human experience. It can only grow from the challenges. When you realize this and begin to live life knowing this, you begin to transcend infertility. You begin to be a better version of yourself than you ever knew you could be. You begin to be a better human.

Action Steps: Creating Balance

Shrinking infertility is all about creating more balance in your life and allowing your internal wisdom to guide decisions and help move you through life's challenges. The task can seem insurmountable when you're so used to focusing on brokenness and the difficulty of infertility. It can seem strange to start planning vacations, going to social events, and clearing out that room that's suppose to be a nursery someday. Creating movement in this way can feel like letting go of the dream of parenthood. Alas, too many of us get stuck and stop creating the movement necessary to grow a family.

Instead, I encourage you to begin creating balance. Creating balance does not mean giving up on your dreams, just as staying stuck does not move you toward your dreams. Instead, shrinking infertility and living all the parts of your life that are important to you help create movement, ease, and peace while still making family-building important. Watch what happens when you begin to notice all these aspects of yourself. Watch yourself realize what you've let float by while you were fixated on the pain of infertility. Then watch yourself open up to more joy, experience, and life.

Exercise 1: Journal Prompts

Get your journal out for this exercise. Please write about all or any of these writing prompts.

- Write about your strengths.
- Find a photo of yourself as a child and talk to yourself in the photo about the things you wish were better in the past and in your current life. What do you want to tell that kid part of you?
- Shrinking IF: Write about all the things you are. All the labels/roles you have. What are the parts about you that you miss? Are there new parts you'd like to add?

- If you had no barriers inherent in infertility, what would you be doing with your life? If you put infertility back in its rightful place (important but not everything), what would be different today?

Exercise 2: Rating Your Mind, Body, and Spirit

Get out your journal; write and complete the following sentences:

In a perfect world, I would rate myself the following on a scale of 1–10 in each of these three areas:

- Mind _____
- Body _____
- Spirit _____

In my actual world, I rate myself the following on a scale of 1–10 in each of these three areas:

- Mind _____
- Body _____
- Spirit _____

What is going well in my actual world in each of these three categories?

What are things I need to do in each category to move toward my perfect world (keeping in mind that perfection is not the ultimate goal; we are wondrous works in progress, and I'm for keeping it that way)?

Fertility Mantra

Practice this mantra in the morning and evening for the next ten days.

Breathing In: Creating a family is important.

Breathing Out: Creating a family isn't everything.

Breathing In: There are many parts of me.

Breathing Out: And I am allowed to live them.

(Repeat three times.)

Fertility Meditation: I Am More Than Infertility

Do this meditation/visualization daily for the next ten days. (Reminder: You can access my recordings of this and all other meditations from this book at www.drmariarothenburger.com/transcendingmeditations.)

Begin by lying down or sitting up in a comfortable position. Eyes closed gently, noticing your breath. Notice the gentle rise and fall of your belly, the expansion and compression of your lungs, and the cool air entering your nostrils, turning warm upon your exhale.

Noticing now all of the tension in your body leaving upon each exhale.

Inhaling, noticing the furrow in your brow completely smooth. Exhaling.

Inhaling, noticing your jaw is completely slack. Exhaling.

Inhaling, noticing your shoulders, arms, and chest are totally loose and free of tension. Exhaling.

Inhaling, letting your stomach out, free to move as you breathe naturally, easily, comfortably. Exhaling.

Inhaling, noticing your legs, calves, ankles, and feet are completely free of tension. Exhaling.

Imagine now you are in a white room. There is nothing here—just clean, empty, white space.

And now, as you look around, you begin to notice various scenes from your life. All of these scenes have to do with infertility. As you look at these scenes, know that if you are uncomfortable at any time, simply open your eyes, and you will be in the present room. Recalling scenes from your fertility journey now, watch objectively as you see yourself, your loved ones, friends, acquaintances, and professionals who are all a part of this journey. You may recall moments of hope and joy. You may also recall moments of deep sorrow. This has been your life for your entire journey to building your family. This room is huge.

Now, you notice a window on the far end of the room. Walking over and looking outside of this room, you notice another room in the shape of a sphere. It's a snow globe! This snow globe is showing another part of your life. A person you used to be, an activity you used to do, or any other part of your life that has been stunted due to fertility issues. What do you see in this snow globe?

Looking to the side of that snow globe is another, and another, and yet another. Hands on the inside of the infertility snow globe, you realize the wall has become viscous, like a bubble. You need only press and you are through the bubble of the snow globe.

On the outside now, you see how large the infertility snow globe is compared to the others. It is at least five times the size. This globe has taken precedence, taken over all the parts of your life. There are many parts of yourself you haven't seen in a long time; perhaps you miss them. Bring one of them to the foreground now. Which snow globe is it? What are you doing? Who are you with? Recall the feelings you had in this moment. Recall what it felt like to be you in that moment.

Bring another snow globe to the forefront. Examine it closely. Which one is it? What are you doing? Who are you with? Recall the feelings of being you in this moment.

Notice for a moment that each time you bring a snow globe to the forefront, the infertility globe shrinks. After noticing the rest of your snow globes around this space—all of the parts of you—notice where the infertility snow globe is.

Wherever it is is completely okay. Perhaps it is in the same position, larger, or smaller—it does not matter. What matters is that you notice. Pay attention to how it feels to see the infertility globe in its current position. What is important about this for your waking life? Is there anything you will change?

[Long pause]

And now, moving your toes, moving your fingers, coming fully back to present. Breathing in, breathing out. Take with you what you noticed about infertility's presence in your life, changing what you will and leaving the rest.

What's Next?

During the course of your healing process, there comes a time when you will begin trusting yourself again. If you're like me, you may have begun putting your trust into professionals and others who mean well and know a lot of things; they're just not you. And only you can determine what's right for you and your mind/body/spirit wellness.

I was recently told by a physician that I should consider going on a particular high-fat diet. I did my due diligence and read the research, hearing what other professionals had to say, and I ultimately decided to try this way of eating. And I did feel better for a bit. However, over time, eating this way did not seem right to me. My body didn't spark with joy when I planned and prepared meals, and knowing what I know now, I decided to eat in a way that made my body happy again.

What I ask folks to do is be a healthy skeptic. I'm not saying to immediately debunk everything you hear, nor am I saying it's necessary to believe everything instantly. I suggest approaching opinions, thoughts, and research (including this book!) in a way that is open to all and attached to nothing. When you're able to approach everything with a sense of curiosity rather than needing an immediate answer and path, you become more in tune with your internal guide. Through this process, you begin learning of your individual needs rather than what a certain statistic says. The following chapter outlines how to begin trusting the inner part of yourself that consistently sends you information about how to thrive in this lifetime.

Chapter Seven

Trust Yourself

*No problem can be solved
from the same level of consciousness that created it.*
— Albert Einstein

You are so much more powerful than you give yourself credit for. Did you know that? Did you know that all your answers lie in wait, eagerly looking forward to the moment when you notice them? Did you know there's a part of you that offers compassion, love, and an all-knowing essence such that you need only state your question, and an answer instantly appears? Did you know you have access to this part of you at any time, in any place, and in any state of mind you wish? It always waits for you. Listening to you and guiding you are its only purpose.

I'm writing this chapter because infertility strips away our ability to remember all of the above. We used to live in a world where we got to decide what happened to us. We got to research that which we didn't know and move forward with our newfound knowledge. Infertility doesn't care about that. You can know all the secrets of the Universe and put them into practice, and infertility will still say, "Um, so? Your cycle is still failing."

And yet...

When you access the part of yourself that already knows all the information you so vehemently seek on Dr. Google, you have an inner knowing, an inner calm, an inner trust that all will be well. When you listen to the part of yourself that actually has the answers instead of some external source that claims to know all, a sense of peace washes over you, and you know that all is—and will be—well, regardless of the outcome of your efforts.

In those moments when you can't access that inner calm (and those moments will arise, as we'll see in the next chapter), you'll still be able to redirect yourself to the awareness that calm is on its way again. It is never far from you. It is, in fact, *you* in the purest sense of the word. It is not your body—this mass of oxygen, carbon, hydrogen, and all the other elements that make up our physical selves. Your body is just a representation of your life on this planet. When I talk about trusting yourself, I mean your Greater Self. The part that comes from Source, God, Yahweh, Nature, whatever you wish to call it. Even atheists have a sense that there is a part of them that is a guidance system. Like, "Um, that dark, dead-end alley doesn't look safe. I think I'll turn around now." Or, "There's just something about that person I really like. Don't know what it is, but I feel like I've known them my whole life." That part of you just knows. That is the part I'm speaking of now.

This chapter is about how I took back the control that infertility had taken from me by paying attention to my own inner awareness of a practical and efficient guidance system that was always—and still is—ready for me at a moment's notice. Spoiler alert: You have access to the same system. Ready to find out how? Let's go.

Meditation and Me

The world hadn't miraculously changed. Our marriage was much, much better through hard work and honoring all our pain. I see that growth as a miracle now, but I didn't see it that way then. We were better because I'd let go, because I'd shrunk IF, I'd stopped "shoulding" on myself, and T had made changes of his own. We grieved Bailey together, we continued healing our relationship, and we continued building our life together without kids.

Damn that was hard. That's why I see our improved marriage as a miracle now. If I had known the miracles to come, I would have been exuberantly looking toward the future. But I'm happy I didn't know. Know why? Because I was forced to stay in the present moment. Minute by minute, hour by hour, day by day…I simply lived. It was the start of a way of being that would change me forever.

At some point after Bailey passed away, I was researching stress reduction when I came across a program out of the University of Massachusetts called Mindfulness-Based Stress Reduction. Curious, I followed the links and read about this program. Now a buzzword, mindfulness was not exceedingly popular at that point, and I didn't know a thing about it until I read Jon Kabat-Zinn's directions on how to do it: "Pay attention in a particular way: on purpose, in the present moment, and non-judgmentally."

"That's it?" I thought. "I can totally do that." And then I tried to do it.

That's when the kicking and screaming began. I was *so bad* at mindfulness meditation! How could anybody be patient enough to do this? What's worse, when I sit and pay attention to the present moment, that's when all the shitty thoughts come back! Where's my blissful state of distraction—you know, that whole "ignorance is bliss" thing? Why can't I just stay distracted and let the terrible thoughts and feelings hang out in the background of my life? Ugh!

I once had a client—years later—tell me she'd had a panic attack while brushing her teeth. "I swear I wasn't even nervous or anything, and I just had a panic attack out of nowhere!"

Yup. That's exactly how it is.

I just knew that meditation was not for me, so I stopped for a while. But dammit if the Universe isn't persistent. I kept being reminded that mindfulness was there, just waiting for me to give it a try. As mentioned earlier, I soon began to see those things as opportunities to prove the research wrong. Mindfulness does *not* work for everyone. Hah! I shall show *you*, research people!

So, I sat. And I got frustrated. And I sat. And I "watched" my stupid breath, and I paid attention to the stupid sounds inside the room and outside the room, and I smelled the stupid smells around me. And, and, and…

Three months later, I got it.

It was only for a fraction of a second. Bliss.

I didn't get rid of my thoughts. But I was able to be aware and objective about them while letting them go. As soon as I was aware that I felt blissful, however, the feeling went away. Still, the experience was exquisite—like coming home after an extended hiatus. It was the opposite of ignorance. It was an all-knowingness, a compassion, a tenderness, a softness that I had never before—not once—felt toward myself.

For the first time ever, I felt what could possibly be self-love. I saw my thoughts as if they were someone else's, and I knew what I would say to a friend with those same thoughts. I was not saying anything helpful to myself. And in that brief millisecond, all I wanted to do was hug that girl who had talked so poorly to herself. After all she'd been through, she was beating herself up on top of it. She didn't deserve it. I didn't deserve it.

> I was not saying anything helpful to myself. And in that brief millisecond, all I wanted to do was hug that girl who had talked so poorly to herself. After all she'd been through, she was beating herself up on top of it. She didn't deserve it. I didn't deserve it.

Once I'd touched upon bliss, my goal changed. I no longer wanted to prove mindfulness wrong. I wanted to find that true bliss again.

After several months of being on the lookout for that blissful state of awareness again (I touched upon it briefly every now and again), I fell into what I call a "zen state." I was in love with life. My marriage was solid, peaceful, and calm again. I had a deep appreciation for who T was, who I was, and who we were together. I had a deep appreciation for the myriad small things in my life. I began delighting in the tiniest of things. That cool new toothpaste flavor that suddenly brought a burst of sensation to my mouth? Yeah, that was worthy of a smile. I came to delight in the fact that I was delighting.

And in that state of being, T and I began to talk about building our family again. He was well past the IVF route that had ravaged our life and relationship.

However, we were still paying a storage fee for frozen embryos, and I didn't feel right destroying them. We talked about transferring our embryos to a new clinic and seeing what they could do to help us.

I loved the new clinic. In sharp contrast to Clinic 1, I felt I was the only patient. They greeted me by name when I walked in. The first time they did that, I turned around thinking someone with the same name must work there and had just walked in. The doc listened to me. He told me to email him, for goodness' sake. Like, when does that happen? And when I did email him, he friggin' emailed back! Almost too good to be true.

We did some additional testing that Clinic 1 had absolutely refused to do. I tested negative for celiac and for natural killer cells. Instead of being frustrated that there was no definitive next treatment protocol, I moved along in an effortless state. The doc encouraged acupuncture and suggested I simply let him know if I began taking herbs again. No big deal. We went forward with the frozen embryo transfer (FET) after transferring the embryos to the new clinic.

In sharp contrast to the hell that was our previous two fresh cycles, I moved through this FET cycle with a smile on my face. I recall once at Clinic 1 when I walked in and saw a patient laughing and joking with a receptionist. A scowl had instantly formed on my face. I thought, "How could she be so disrespectful? How could she dare laugh at a time like this? People are trying to make babies without sex, here, people! Be solemn, dammit!"

Well, I was that smiling, calm, laughing patient now. I was in love with life and simply going with the flow. I saw beauty in everything—the gentle fragrance of the waiting area, the cushiness of the chairs, the silence, the shape of the friggin' magazine rack. I mean, beauty was everywhere!

Instead of seeing anything as a barrier, I began to honor it for its opportunities. Slow person in front of me on the way to the clinic? Hmm, I must need to slow down. I have to wait an extra fifteen minutes to see the doc? Hmm, I must need to rest a bit more. All the while, I'm thinking, "Who is this person? Am I crazy? If so, then crazy feels good. I think I'll just hang out here a bit longer."

I'll never forget the day they transferred our precious embryos back to my uterus. I'd begun the progesterone in oil (PIO) shots my body hated so much. For some reason, PIO shots were fine going in, even though the needles were gigantic to let the oil pass through into the hindquarters. But afterward? Yeah, that was hell. I had a hard time even sitting down at times. When I had to lie down on the gurney, I yelped because the PIO shots had punched me in the ass and upper thighs, causing bruises to take up residence on the white background of my skin. Yes, it was painful, but it was also kind of artistic. I actually made a joke about it, and the nurse laughed as she led me down the hall.

Inside the room where they would transfer our little babies, I assumed the position that any girl at a gynecologist's office is familiar with: spread eagle in stirrups, nothing on below my waist-length paper gown other than my super lucky transfer socks. Nurses, medical assistants, and the embryologist walked around me, casually chatting as if all was normal and good with the world. And it was.

The nurse came into the room and hesitatingly asked, "Um, did T get an AIDS panel done?" We answered in the affirmative. Long pause. "Well, we don't have it yet, and we can't do the transfer until it shows clear. I'll call and get it. It's going to be at least fifteen more minutes."

With my vagina practically flailing in the wind, just awaiting that lovely catheter full of my embryos, the bruises on my backside began screaming at me to get off them. On top of that, my bladder—already full to the max (as it should be for proper transfer)—felt like it was about to burst. Fortunately, another nurse popped in to ask, "Do you want to go to the bathroom and let a little out?"

Question: How the heck does anybody let just a little out? I mean, is that even within the realm of possibility? Nonetheless, wondering how I could get up off the gurney without a little leaking out, I gratefully replied that I would indeed let a little out.

Just looking back at this part of my cycle, I realize that I was so calm, collected, happy even—so different from how I'd been during previous cycles. To be completely honest, I'd never been as cool a cucumber as I was that day. I rolled with all the bumps. All of them. Even the one coming.

This FET was the only cycle I got pregnant. My beta test (blood test for pregnancy) came back positive at a 25. That is not high, but the embryo could have implanted late.

When the second test came back that there was no doubling, the doc informed me he thought I was having a chemical pregnancy. Of course, we were hopeful and went in for a third test, which confirmed the chemical pregnancy. A miscarriage.

I wept. I'd had a ton of hope for that cycle, even though I had no expectation.

This grief was different, though. Historically, I would rage for a few hours before the grief set in and then I'd become a shadow of myself for weeks. This time, however, after twenty-four hours of sadness, I walked down the narrow, carpeted steps of our little Cape Cod starter home, turned the corner into the tiny kitchen, gathered all the needles and remaining drugs on the counter, and swept them right into the garbage.

This is not the safe way to dispose of those items. A "good" person would use a sharps container rather than a typical household waste bin. But I didn't give a fuck. Not one single fuck. You know why?

I WAS FREE!

It was like I was moving around in slow motion and gleefully getting rid of all the paraphernalia that had kept me trapped in infertility land for the last six and a half years. Every single reminder was tossed into the garbage along with the thousands of tears I'd shed in my prison, stagnant with the weight of my dreams not coming true.

I no longer felt that my dreams weren't coming true. Instead, I was creating them in that moment. I was free.

My doc practically begged me to go back to the clinic. He wanted to work on my egg quality. The old, desperate me would have easily been moved back into the treatment world. Actually, I never would have left. But now I was an entirely new person.

Listen up, because this part is very important: In the words of Joseph Campbell, I was following my bliss. I knew following the doc's recommendations was not my bliss. It's not just that I knew it with my brain; I felt it in my soul. Treatments were not the way to parenthood.

I didn't know what lay around the corner of our lives. But I did know that my dreams were going to come true and that I'd have to move away from the medical community. It's scary, don't you think? Here's this very powerful community telling you precisely what you need to do next, and you reply, "No, thanks. My bliss is this direction." Your bliss? Yeah, okay, crazy lady. Did you light a candle, sage your room, and read your tarot cards too?

The point is, Scary will always be there. Scary is all up in our business every single friggin' day. And when you choose to look Scary in the face, give it a hug, and do whatever it is you want to do anyway, you will have run straight into your courage. The more you tune in to your intuition, trust what you have to say is your next move, acknowledge the fear, give it a hug, and make your next move anyway, the more content, powerful, and peaceful you'll be.

I knew that my next move was to walk away from treatments. I felt it. And by this point—after all the years of suffering—I finally trusted myself.

Fertility Key: Trust Yourself

Have you ever had that thing where you think of someone, then they send you a text message? Before caller ID (BCID) you would have been able to pick up the ringing phone and say, "Hi, Bill. Yeah, for some reason I knew it was you." Perhaps someone has made that comment when you called or texted them. "OMG, I was just thinking of you!" What about that phrase "trust your gut"? You've heard that before, right? It's that feeling that makes you think twice before walking down a dark alley at night. It's more than just thinking "Hey, it's dark, I'm alone, and that's a possibly unsafe alley. Don't walk there." It's a literal sensation in your body that tells you that walking down the alley is bad idea. In both of these examples, you trust yourself, don't you? You know that what your body is telling you is true.

But what happens when you have a gut feeling about something that is the complete opposite of what you think should happen? What happens when everyone around you is telling you something that your body tells you is not right for you? My doctor pressed me hard to continue treatments; he had many studies and reasoned very well that I could possibly conceive and carry to term under his care. Years prior, I would have been sucked right in despite the discomfort. I may have even shrugged off the sensations as nerves, jitters, or "cold feet." But this time, I payed attention to my Inner Guide. As scary as that was, I knew I could trust it now.

This fertility key is to help you begin to trust yourself again too. Everyone is born with the ability to intuit; it's a way to keep us safe, to keep us on the right path for us. Sure, others may benefit from that new fad diet or amazing new exercise machine or that just-new-on-the-market fertility treatment that comes with a set of Ginsu knives. But will you? Nobody in the world can tell you what will work for you, regardless of the research, what worked for others, or what statistics are in your favor. You know why? Because *you* are the boss of you. Only you get to guide yourself toward your ultimate goals. Knowing that you can trust your intuition—your instinct—is quite scary at first. After all, you've likely been used to reasoning, logic, statistics, professional opinions, and—ahem—Dr. Google to make "informed" decisions. And yes, this type of reasoning is quite useful. There's nothing wrong with looking at data. The problem comes when we listen to all this reasoning, our bodies and intuition still emit something-isn't-quite-right signals, and we ignore said signals. In this fertility key, I'm asking you to get out of your head and into your intuition. What's the difference, you ask? Excellent question!

If you're like me, you just want to know stuff, don't you? You want to know next steps, know whether to pursue a treatment, know whether to attend a party or not, or know what kind of exercise or food is right for you. When I talk about knowing in this chapter, I mean the idea of an immediate knowing. This is the kind of knowing that does not require the typical pros-and-cons lists, Excel spreadsheets, and hours of research. Reason and intellect are useful, of course, but when we balance them out with knowing from a higher space, we become even more productive and efficient.

Here's a metaphor for you. Imagine you're standing in front of a giant wall. It's as tall as you can see up and as wide as you can see on either side of you. You have to get to the other side. Infertility feels just like this, doesn't it? Using your reason and logic, you may surmise many things. Perhaps you decide the wall is too large, so you simply give up and turn around. Maybe you decide you can scale it, so you go about the task of gathering the necessary tools and supplies. You could also decide to keep walking either left or right, hoping for an opening somewhere. Or perhaps there's a way to dig underneath! All of these are reasonable pursuits, but it's incredibly difficult to know which one to move toward. Now imagine that you're able to float above the wall. From this vantage point, you're able to see where you are, where the wall is, and what's beyond the wall. This is like intuition! Because you're now so high off the ground, you're also able to see an efficient way to get to the other side. Using all your resources, logic, reason, and intuition, you're able to devise a plan that's the best for you.

What would your fertility journey be like if you were able to access your intuition? What would be different for you? How much stress relief would you have if you instantly knew what to do next? You have all the resources within you to access this knowing! We all do! And when you begin to become aware of, cultivate, and practice using your intuition, you'll begin to realize that you can trust yourself at all times.

Pineal Gland

Located behind the middle of the forehead, about two-thirds of the way toward the back of the brain and above the brain stem, is a tiny, pinecone-shaped structure called the pineal gland. It is the structure responsible for balancing the circadian rhythm in the body by producing melatonin—a hormone necessary for quieting the body and brain for sleep.

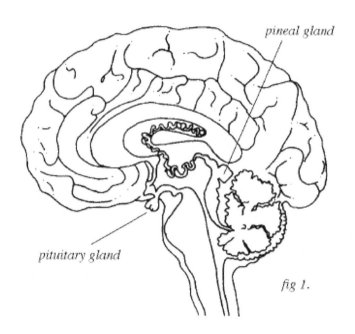

fig 1.

The pineal is also often referred to as "the third eye." Ancient Hindu teachings link the sixth chakra to the pineal gland, which is the way to access higher "seeing" or knowing. Interestingly, the chamber the pineal gland sits in is lined with structures called pinealocytes, which are similar to the rods and cones in the retina of the eye and are wired to the visual cortex of the brain just as the eyes are, so pinealocytes are quite literally a third eye. I mention this gland here because many ancient-wisdom and mystical teachings discuss the activation of the pineal gland as a beautiful way to intuition and wisdom. Activating this gland is like the metaphor of floating above the Infertility Wall and seeing your path to the other side. You'll practice activating this gland with the meditation assigned for this chapter.

HeartMath

In the world of fertility issues, it's helpful to find a balance between thinking and feeling (or intuiting)—a balance between knowing with your mind and knowing with your heart. Perhaps no one has explored this topic more extensively than the HeartMath Institute (HMI), an organization dedicated to researching the capabilities of the human heart. Over several decades, HMI's studies have shown that within the heart are neuron-like cells called neurites that, like the brain, can actually think and communicate with other parts of the body. Not only that, the heart seems to intuitively "know" certain things even before the brain does (by a second or slightly more). HMI's research supports the notion that intuition (which they define as "the process of perceiving or knowing things to a high degree of certainty without conscious reasoning") is more than one organ's reception of information; rather, measurable changes take place in the entire body, and the heart seems to play a central role.

The heart has an electromagnetic field emanating from it that is measurable up to three feet outside the body. This field is able to give and receive information from the fields of others and from the energetic field all around us. This is why you might be able to tell what someone is feeling, even if you have no way of knowing this through what you perceive with your five senses (e.g., seeing tears or hearing cries). Your body has a physical reaction to intuitive perception, so it's almost like you're feeling these emotions yourself.

HeartMath scientists focus on what's called heart-rhythm coherence. Essentially, when your heart rhythms are coherent, they can be measured by

HMI's biofeedback technology as very smooth and ordered. When one's heart is incoherent, the rhythm would be shown as jagged and chaotic. Researchers have linked heart coherence to the ability to receive intuitive information, the reversal of stress-chemical pathways, and optimal mental clarity due to increased heart-brain communication.

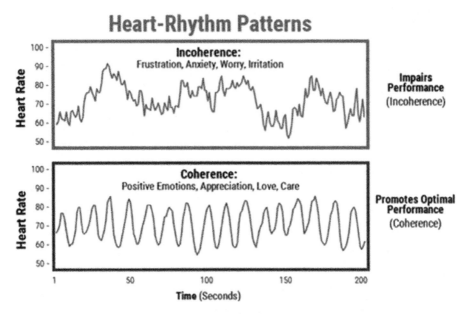

(Courtesy of HeartMath Institute)

So, how can heart-rhythm coherence be useful for you in your journey to parenthood? I'll give you an example. When my doctor encouraged me to begin another cycle, insisting he could help with my egg quality, he was sending information to me with his words and what he was feeling or emoting inside. My heart electromagnetic field received that information, and I had a physical reaction to the information based on what was right for me. If it had resonated with me, I may have had a positive reaction. Instead, the HeartMath Institute would say my heart rhythms became incoherent, meaning I had a negative reaction and knew intuitively that another cycle was not for me. In this case, I listened to my intuition and ignored my thoughts about what it would take to begin another cycle.

Think of what that would mean for your journey. Do you often go back and forth about what to do next? Do you wonder about types of treatment? No treatment? Adoption? What to do in relationships? Whether or not to attend a baby shower? Should you buy that cute little baby blanket? The questions are daily if not hourly, and they consume quite a bit of headspace, don't you think? What if you didn't need to attend to the nuisance of decision-making like this anymore? How much more relaxed would you be? How much more could you kick anxiety to the curb? How much more could you do the things you actually want to be doing? Popcorn and a Netflix binge, anyone? Or how about ignoring that baby shower invitation and going on a day-long hike? Decision-making completely free of guilt because you would know in your heart it's the right thing for you. This way of accessing your intuition is literally deciding your next moves based on your heart's content.

One giant bonus that is seriously helpful on your fertility journey: Being in heart coherence triggers cell repair throughout the body. Say what?! Yes, my friend, you can begin to heal your body when you practice being in a state of heart coherence. That means subfertility, unexplained infertility, and other types of infertility can all be healed without medical intervention. That's saying a lot, I know, and I'm certainly not advocating for you to stop any treatments you're currently utilizing. I am saying that this is a wonderful complement to the treatment that's already working for you (if it is indeed working for you). I frequently mention that my own self-healing included completely eliminating my symptoms of endometriosis (a disease the medical community states is incurable) as well as experiencing spontaneous vision improvement (which perplexed my doctors, since they believed that my vision should have been getting worse with age). As with all things in this book, however, I encourage you to do your own research and draw your own conclusions.

A final important note on intuition: It's instantaneous. Intuitive knowing requires no thought from the brain. In fact, thinking with the brain feels clunky and dense by comparison. Thinking with the brain begins to feel like those dreams where you're trying to run in water or mud; ever have one of those? You might eventually get to where you're headed, but dang, it's slow and frustrating! Thinking with the heart doesn't involve any mud. There are no pros-and-cons lists. There are no graphs and charts. There's no research. You simply know in an instant. Can you imagine that? If nothing else, listening to your intuition is a major time-saver. And who doesn't want that?

Loving Your Body

I'm taking a moment here to acknowledge something inherently difficult when dealing with fertility issues: being okay with your body. Even if you've never struggled with body-image issues, fertility issues can bring up a whole host of body judgments, especially when your body is the source of the problem. Accessing your intuition can feel quite scary, because I'm asking you to pay close attention to your body sensations. This is a skill you've gotten quite good at while trying to conceive, perhaps not in a pleasant way. Every flutter, ache, tingle, pain, craving, mood change, headache, or other bodily sensation is accounted for. You notice the smallest detail of every moment in your body when trying to conceive, and when things don't work out well, noticing details can become quite upsetting.

> Even if you've never struggled with body-image issues, fertility issues can bring up a whole host of body judgments, especially when your body is the source of the problem.

The problem is, we tend to decipher each signal as one problem or another, get on Dr. Google to research it, and continue to have angst because of the overwhelming amount of inconclusive information out there; then we're right back to not trusting ourselves. When a cycle doesn't work out or our bodies don't respond to intervention like we'd hoped, we tend to be very hard on our bodies. We note the ways in which we hate them and can't stand being in them. If this resonates, I'm with you, and I'm sending you loads of loving kindness right this very moment.

This chapter's Fertility Mantra is geared toward healing your body image and loving your body. And the Action Steps are designed to help you develop your intuition and begin trusting your body again as well as your Higher Self. I suspect that you've already had a great deal of practice with this if you've had to deal with fertility issues; but even if you're starting from the beginning, approach it with a fun and curious attitude. And as always, seek the help of a professional if this becomes overwhelming to handle on your own.

Action Steps: Accessing Intuition

By now you've been through several weeks of meditation, which means you're getting good at getting silent. Getting silent is probably one of the most important baseline skills for accessing your intuition since the quiet is what helps us tune in to what our intuition is actually saying. I have a sign in my office now that says, "The quieter you are, the more you hear." This is true with all relationships and is great for improving communication, but in this context, I'm referring to listening to your Self. Accessing your intuition is like tuning in to your Greater, Wiser Self—the part of you that has a bird's-eye view of your life and can help guide you like a chess player moving pieces along a board. This is why meditation is so important in this program. Way back in the first chapter, I wrote that the internet told me to pray a lot. Hindsight tells me I needed to meditate a lot. Have you heard the saying "Prayer is like talking to God; meditation is like listening for the answer"? Accessing intuition is listening for the answer from your own source of wisdom.

As mentioned in this chapter's Fertility Key section, knowing via intuition is instantaneous. There's no brain chatter to deal with, making this the quickest way to have an answer for any problem you may be dealing with on your journey. The exercises below are designed to help you learn what basic intuition feels like, then we move to strengthening intuition and finally to a meditation to activate the pineal gland and access intuition from a deeper state.

> Knowing via intuition is instantaneous. There's no brain chatter to deal with, making this the quickest way to have an answer for any problem you may be dealing with on your journey.

Exercise 1: Get Familiar with Your Intuition

This is a deceptively simple practice for beginning to learn what your internal guidance system feels like. You've probably felt this many times over the course of your life but never really paid attention to the physical sensations or the emotions produced. For this exercise, either record your own voice or have someone say these words to you:

Yes. (Repeat three times.)

No. (Repeat three times.)

After hearing the word *yes* three times, notice what it feels like in your body to feel that word. Write those sensations down. Then notice what emotions come up when you hear that word. Do the same for the word *no*. Again, this exercise is deceptively simple. There are often nuances that are difficult to put into words; don't get too caught up in not being able to name the sensations or feelings you're experiencing. The main point of this exercise is for you to get familiar with your personal guidance system. You'll be able to use your familiarity with these sensations in future exercises and with decision-making in general. The rest of the exercises in this chapter are designed to help you put this simple yes/no exercise into play in the real world.

Exercise 2: Try on the Jeans Technique

Have you ever been in a dressing room trying on jeans? Finding that perfect pair is like striking gold; I almost have to stop myself from shouting out loud, "Eureka!" when I've found a near-perfect fit. In order to get to that great fit, though, there are a lot of pairs of jeans to go through, aren't there? It's rare that plucking a pair of jeans off the shelf produces immediately satisfying results in the changing room (unless you've bought them before, of course).

This technique is like trying on those jeans. You know the sensation of trying on a pair of jeans that doesn't fit right. Either they really don't fit, or they kind of sort of fit, but not really. This is the equivalent of *no* in the previous exercise. And you know what it feels like to try on a pair of jeans that fits really well. It's like angels start singing, right? I can hear those angels now. Those jeans are snug and loose in all the right places. This is the equivalent of *yes* in the previous exercise.

What if making decisions was like trying on a pair of jeans? What if you could know almost instantly what decision is right for you? Sure, you could bring up all those color-coded spread sheets, pros-and-cons lists, and interviews with professionals. But what if you could save yourself all that work and have an instant knowing of what direction is best for you?

For this exercise, I'm going to ask you to play a bit. Get out of your head and into your heart for this; create a really fun mindset and get super curious about what's happening. Start by taking a walk, hopping on your bike, or getting into your car. You don't need to have a destination in mind, but in the beginning it could be useful. (Returning home? Getting gas? Going to a friend's home?) When you get really good at playing, you won't need the end goal. You'll be curious to see what comes up.

Okay, so now that you're in your chosen mode of transport, you want to make sure to not have any distractions. No headphones, no phone—just you and the activity. Once you begin moving and have warmed up to the notion that you're just going to play for the next few minutes, begin to ask yourself, "Which direction should I go? Right? Left? Straight?"

Remember the sensations of *yes* and *no*? This is where that skill comes in very handy. You're trying on the jeans here. "Try on" turning left and ask yourself what it feels like. "Try on" turning right and ask yourself what it feels like, and so on. The idea is to go with the *yes* choice, but after a while it may be fun to go with the *no* choice and see what happens.

One caveat: Just like when trying on jeans, there is rarely a time when there is an absolute perfect fit. Even when the jeans hug my thighs perfectly and there's no gap around my waist, they may be too long. That's the beauty of intuition, there are a million little nuances. In this case, go with the jeans that feel the best. So, when you're on your practice journey in this exercise, sometimes you'll notice that none of the directions feel exactly right. If they all feel exactly the same, then choose the one that comes first to your attention. More often than not, though, you'll notice that there are differences. Choose the one that feels the lightest. Most of all, have fun with this exercise! If you notice you're not having fun and you're feeling a little anxious, it's time to remind yourself to get out of your head and into your heart. The next exercise will help you do just that.

Exercise 3: Get into Your Heart

This simple exercise (taken straight from HeartMath Institute) is called "The Quick Coherence Technique." It's a way to practice what it feels like to think from your heart rather than from your head. You can access this technique video online as well (https://www.heartmath.com/quick-coherence-technique/). The exercise involves two steps and takes only a minute or two:

1. Focus your attention on the area of your heart. Imagine you can breathe from your heart space. Inhale and exhale in a rhythm that's comfortable for you, making the breaths long and slow (e.g., inhale for five seconds, exhale for five seconds, repeat).
2. Recall a pleasant memory. This can be of someone you love, a favorite place, a pleasant interaction, a pet, or anything else that feels like appreciation, gratitude, or caring.

Continue this exercise for a minute or two (or more if you wish).

One fantastic thing about this exercise is that it brings your heart into coherence while you're engaging in the exercise, but the coherence lasts even beyond that. This is a wonderful way to not only practice what it's like being in your heart space but to set a tone for the rest of your day and to continue developing your intuition.

Fertility Mantra

Practice this mantra on body love for the next ten days in the morning and in the evening.

Breathing in: I am whole.

Breathing out: My body is perfect exactly how it is.

Breathing in: I trust my body to guide me.

Breathing out: I can access and trust my intuition.

(Repeat three times.)

Fertility Meditation: Accessing Intuition

Do this meditation for the next ten days. (Reminder: You can access my recordings of this and all other meditations from this book at www.drmariarothenburger.com/transcendingmeditations.)

This meditation is designed to calm your body and mind such that you will find your inner guide. Intuition is not thought. It is not emotion. It is an inner knowing that brings about a sense of strong peace. You can access this part of yourself at any time; this meditation will help you begin to become familiar with this part of you.

Begin by sitting in a comfortable position, hands on knees or in your lap. You may also lie down; if you are tired, however, and at risk of falling asleep, consider sitting up for this meditation.

Deeply and slowly inhale to the count of five. Exhale to the count of five. Repeat this three times. Now, place your hand on your belly. Notice your belly rise and fall.

Body scanning down to calm.

Now...feel where your head is in space, be it laying on a pillow or floating in space as if pulled by an imaginary thread up into the sky. In your mind's eye, envision the space between your brows. This area of your forehead is called *Ajna* in Sanskrit, or the third eye.

It is the area that, when perfectly balanced and aligned with your greatest self, becomes the area where you access full-spectrum knowing, intuition, insight, and wisdom. Accessing this space within allows you to evaluate yourself without judgment, create openness to ideas, learn from experience, and foster emotional intelligence.

Accessing this space, you are able see more clearly, not with your eyes but *through* your eyes. And you begin to develop a deep and calm inner awareness of what your next steps are in any given situation.

As you notice this space between your brows, become aware of a slowly pulsing indigo light the size of a tiny hole in a sewing needle. This tiny light is undulating its way larger and larger as you watch.

The indigo light is softly glowing, undulating, and now you can see it spinning freely, as if it is a little dark-blue pinwheel. Now it's about the size of a golf ball, and you imagine its radiant light making its way through your forehead into your brain, lighting it up.

The light is making its way to the very center of your brain, right behind your third-eye chakra, where it comes into contact with the pinecone-shaped pineal gland about two-thirds of the way through the center of your brain. The light stays there for a bit, giving extra attention to this gland, which is your intuitive center. Your pineal gland wakes up, and therefore your intuition is now alive with energy.

The light now grows larger and larger, encompassing first your head, then grows until it encompasses your whole body. It holds you lightly, securely, and with warmth.

Now in your imagination, notice you are standing on a gravel path. You'll notice the trees lining the road, and the dappling of the sunlight on the ground. There is a light breeze touching your skin; it's the perfect temperature.

As you stroll, you notice the smell of fresh-cut grass, hear a little brook nearby, and see birds flitting around in the trees. This is a pleasant space for you, and you realize how perfectly calm your body is. Perhaps there is the smallest smile on your lips, demonstrating the peace you feel.

You continue to stroll, noticing the surrounding nature, when ahead you see a change in the road. As you get closer, you realize it is a fork in the road.

A sign between the two paths indicates a choice you must make. See what the sign says. What is the decision you are faced with?

In this space, decision-making is kept simple, and we are only looking at two of the possibilities for this particular instance. What are the two choices you are considering?

Which one is on the left?

Which one is on the right?

Now...move closer to the choice on the right. Without judgment, simply notice the sensations that arise when you consider this particular choice. Does it feel positive? Negative? A mixture of the two?

Now...move back to the center, looking at both choices. And move closer to the one on the left. Without judgment, notice how this choice feels. What sensations arise as you consider this particular choice? Are the sensations negative? Positive? A mixture?

Now, move back to the center of the road again, looking at both choices. Recall how you felt about the first choice. Recall how you felt about the second choice. Which one feels lighter? Easier? More positive or even more neutral?

If they feel similar, that is okay. You can always try this exercise again tomorrow. For now, notice the thoughts that come up as you do this visualization; watch them move away as you concentrate on your inner guide, your greater self that always knows what is in your best interest. It's like floating above a brick wall; you can clearly see what is on the other side, and which path to take.

And now...make your way back to your present space. Take a deep inhale and blow it all away. Wiggle your fingers, wiggle your toes. And when you're ready, flutter your eyes open.

What's Next?

The previous chapters have helped you focus on getting quiet, having a more fertile mindset, living life more fully, and engaging spiritual connection by activating your intuition. But what happens when the shit hits the fan again? And it will. Even though you've developed a calmer way of being, difficult moments can still hurt. Being human, we want to run away from pain, particularly if it's reminiscent of past trauma. Too often we succeed in abating the pain for a while, but it dutifully shows up again and again—sometimes with more vigor—until we face it and resolve it. The next chapter is about handling the hard stuff well, with grace, ease, and peace.

Chapter Eight

Be the Bamboo

Fall down seven times, stand up eight.
— Japanese Proverb

Back when I was voraciously seeking any information to help me feel better about my inability to conceive, I came across a little book that changed my viewpoint tremendously. It took many years to put the concepts into practice because I simply wasn't ready to let go of attempting to control the universe. In the pages of this book, I found the concept of moving with the tides and storms that life inevitably throws our way. It was a concept about moving through difficulty with more ease, less angst, and greater present awareness. I realized the value of this immediately, and I began looking for evidence that this mindset—this way of being—was real. Following is a blog post I wrote about "Being the Bamboo."

When I worked in the mortgage industry, I had the good fortune to work with a wonderful loan officer. A gentle giant among type-A, narcissistic, anxiety-driven maniacs, CB was (and probably still is) a breath of fresh air.

One time I had to tell CB that I'd screwed up one of his loans. Expecting a lecture fraught with anger and loathing (or at the very least a scowl), I was stunned into wide-eyed silence when CB turned to me and calmly said, "Well…it is what it is," and left it at that.

The power of that statement is much more profound than the actual words. To be sure, it means various things to different people. To me, it meant, "It's not your fault. It simply is." Wow.

I'm currently reading *The Way of the Fertile Soul* by Randine Lewis. She gives many tools for diagnosing an emotional problem via the Tao (literally, the Way), a traditional Chinese way of being. Many blockages are identified via emotions like impatience, hatred, victimization, grief, low self-worth, etc. I've come to recognize that I have several of these emotions floating around in me. Namely, resistance, frustration, feeling powerless, fear, and low self-worth.

I don't feel victimized in the least…I feel my infertility is my fault. I did something in my life that caused me to be infertile. As a result, I'm pissed at myself, and I'm resistant to being gentle and compassionate with myself. Per the Tao, the only thing that is faulty is my thinking.

Randine Lewis describes the workings of the world as just that: the workings of the world. I imagine CB would say, "Well, Maria…they are what they are."

Lewis also illustrates human nature within the workings of the world. She says that if you consider a rigid tree in the midst of a hurricane, you may see it snapping and falling over, causing more damage. Flexible trees, like bamboo, flow and move with the wind. As she puts it, "Because we cannot change or stop the wind, it's essential to move with the inevitable changes that blow through our lives."

All those years ago, a gentle giant taught me a lesson, and only now am I beginning to utilize that teaching. Thus continues my healing journey: I must not blame myself.

Infertility is the wind, and I am the bamboo.

An Example of Not Being the Bamboo

Flash back to when I couldn't handle hard shit. Just before our first IVF cycle, I was super excited because I just knew that this time it was going to work. After all the crap the Universe had put us through, this was our time. I mean, damn, I did every single little thing I was told to do (thanks, Dr. Google). Plus, my friend just down the street—the one whom I'd been walking our dogs with almost every morning for the last year—was now pregnant with her first child after her very first IVF. Obviously, that could happen for me, too, right? Right?!

I recall the day we got the news of how our cycle turned out. After settling down from the initial tantrum, the heartbreak began to create a crack in my fragile psyche. Normally, a morning walk with a friend would be an activity soothing for the soul. But she was pregnant. And I was not. Things had changed.

She was sad for me, to be sure. She said all the placations a good friend should say, yet I could have sworn I detected an undercurrent of thank-god-that-didn't-happen-to-me. After her pregnancy began showing, our morning walks became more than uncomfortable for me. And our conversations reflected the discomfort. Walking alongside each other, we talked about everything from the weather to our jobs and spouses. We talked about our dogs' latest antics, trips to the vet, and flea-and-tick treatments. But we avoided pregnancy talk like the plague. I thought she was being sensitive. Come to find out, she thought I was being insensitive.

I discovered some time later that she had been perusing my anonymous blog. She read a post I put on there about how sorry I was that I could not be a typical friend asking about one's pregnancy. If I did, I felt I may have exploded. Knowing what I know now, if I were the pregnant one in a duo like this, I would make it known that my friend would not need to ask a single question. Not one question! Even though we both went through this together, I know that I would be understanding enough to not require a single conversation about my pregnancy.

That is not how this person felt.

She was pissed. I was uninvited to the baby shower (thank god!), though I left a gift on her doorstep (a hand-crocheted baby blanket that took me months to create, likely fueled by the guilt of not being able to talk about her baby). She stopped talking to me. We stopped being friends. It was an absolute breakup. And I did not take it well.

On one hand, I was relieved that I wouldn't need to see her belly grow continuously. On the other hand, I was angry and sad that I had misjudged her. I felt stupid that guilt consumed me due to my inability to speak about her pregnancy, and she was not gracious about this at all. I felt kicked when I was down.

Were I able to notice that this was part of the shit that inevitably happens in life, I may have been able to move through it like a bamboo tree on the receiving end of a strong windstorm. Instead, I snapped. I became angry, bitter, and resentful. Guilt no longer consumed me; in its place were proverbial daggers thrown at her at any chance I got. I wished terrible things on her, and, as I have often said to clients, I completely understand if you've had these thoughts, too. It's not pathological. It's coming from a place of deep pain and loss.

The Orange Theory

In one of my favorite analogies, Wayne Dyer asked his audiences, "If you squeeze an orange, what comes out?" Inevitably, an audience member would answer, "Orange juice!" Dr. Dyer would then ask, "Why?" After some tittering and silliness, the audience would come to the conclusion, "Because that's what's inside."

Dr. Dyer would then go on to ask what happens if you are the one being squeezed (metaphorically). What if someone cuts you off on the highway, makes fun of you, calls you a name, or degrades you? What comes out of you? Is it bitterness? Hatred? Resentment? Anger? Daggers? If so, why? Because that's what's inside.

Does it matter who does the squeezing? No. Does it matter the implement with which you're squeezed? No. None of that matters. All that matters is what's inside.

Now, by the same logic, if what we cultivate within ourselves is peacefulness, joy, abundance, ease, and love, that's what will come out. It doesn't mean that difficult times aren't painful, but the response to the pain is quite different.

> If what we cultivate within ourselves is peacefulness, joy, abundance, ease, and love, that's what will come out. It doesn't mean that difficult times aren't painful, but the response to the pain is quite different.

This is what it means to be the bamboo. We move with the pain, we acknowledge its existence. And we move on, all the while treating ourselves and others with the kindness and compassion we all deserve.

Had I been cultivating peace within myself when this situation with my former friend transpired, I know there would have been a different response. I would have grieved, I would have let her go, and I would have wished her nothing but peace. I may have recognized that our friendship had served its purpose and that it no longer served either one of us.

This chapter is about cultivating the ability to move through such pain with a sense of ease. Let me be clear, moving through challenging situations does not mean there is no pain. You will experience pain. You will experience heartbreak. You will experience a deep sense of loss and utter exhaustion. The difference is, once the storm has passed, you'll stop living in the storm and start living in the present. Eventually, all storms move on.

Our parenthood journey continues with an excellent example of a time in my "zen" headspace that I was able to "be the bamboo." This is in stark contrast to the intense difficulty of previous painful experiences during infertility, and you can experience this ability, too.

The Adoption Road

At this point, I knew T and I were going to be child free. We had talked about it, and I had already begun planning the many travels we'd be having through our retirement and the rest of our lives together. I was already thinking about larger property for our future six dogs and all the ways in which I could move forward in my career, never having to worry about motherhood. It was a very real choice we were making to live child free, and I couldn't have been happier.

Two weeks later and many vacations already planned in my head, T changed his mind. "I really want to be a dad," he said. Now, the old Maria would have likely been pissed. We had a solid plan and goals for moving forward with life—why change them?! The new me was not pissed. I was taking everything as it came my way and deciding what to do with it on the spot. I was so content with the way life was, I didn't resist, I wasn't rigid, and

I didn't throw a tantrum. I simply accepted everything as it entered into my awareness.

The new me said, "Okay, honey, no problem. Let's look at adoption." And just as fervently and passionately as I had planned our future child-free vacations, I researched and (mostly joyfully) looked at our adoption options. I was all about this zen-living-in-the-moment thang! Woot!

Now, you know that thing when people give unsolicited advice about what to do about infertility? Among the first sentences is generally, "Well, why don't you just adopt?" Aside from the silly idea that adoption is a kind of replacement for the very real grief that one experiences at not being able to conceive and carry a child, the word "just" is totally misguiding. It implies "Infertility is hard. Go with adoption—it's so much easier!"

I'm here to tell you, nothing—nothing—could be further from the truth. Adoption is hard. In fact, I think infertility and the resultant headspace I was in was the perfect preparation for the process. I don't know how I would've fared if I'd still been crazy. If you're in the middle of your fertility journey and looking at adoption as an option, I'm confirming your fears that it's like starting from square one. It has its own challenges, worries, and pitfalls, though to discuss the entirety of the journey is beyond the scope of this book. Bottom line: If you decide to pursue adoption and you follow all the keys listed in this book, you will be able to handle it. Shoot, you've dealt with infertility; you've proven you can do hard things.

As T put it, he would've been happy with an alien baby. I was a little more interested in a human baby—not to be picky. So I started checking out particular adoption programs and seeing what we could qualify for here on Earth.

There are a lot of ways one can adopt, including foster care, domestic private adoption, international adoption, and adoption of a family member. T and I knew we didn't want a domestic (US) private adoption, primarily because I was trusting my intuition that it wasn't the right avenue for us. There were several other reasons, though, not the least of which is feeling fearful of a birth parent deciding to parent after we had our hearts set on the precious baby coming into our home. Make no mistake, we believe that the best place for a child is with their biological family. Period. I just didn't think my heart could handle another loss as big as that, and I trusted my gut with every ounce of my being. We needed to adopt internationally.

This is no small feat either. First, we had to choose an agency and look into their programs. On one occasion, I told T about an agency in NYC that was holding a seminar to learn about their international adoption programs. I had always been drawn to Asian countries' culture, values, and customs, and I was particularly interested in Korean adoption because I'd heard their foster-care and medical-care systems are outstanding. So we went to the evening seminar, looking forward to beginning our (second) journey to our baby. As we sat listening to the speaker, some content popped up that I could not wrap my brain around: Those who had been to therapy or had taken antidepressant medication within the last two years weren't eligible to adopt from Korea, according to this program. I thought, "Are you kidding me?" I'm a psychotherapist! What the heck would they think of my profession, for god's sake?

Not believing my ears, I went up to the presenters at the end of the talk and asked my specific question. Yes, it was okay that I was a therapist. Yes, it was okay that I went to therapy, if I got a letter from my therapist saying it was due to infertility and not due to a psychiatric condition. No, it was not okay that T had taken antidepressants during the time we were knocking on divorce's door.

I was astounded. And I walked away from that evening wondering if we had to be perfect in order to be parents. All the old infertility thoughts surfaced, and I felt the weight of those thoughts as if they'd never left my psyche.

But because I'd been training my brain to go with the flow, I felt my pain, I held T's hand, and we went for a slice of New York pizza. We were both incredibly disappointed, and we were okay. It was one of those lovely NYC nights, a little dampness in the air, the glorious smell of garlic knots wafting by our eager nostrils, a small table, thin-crust pizza slices, and each other. We were okay. And we would be okay for the rest of our lives, no matter what. If infertility didn't take us down, this little ol' adoption agency shaking their shaming finger at us offered barely a scratch on the ironclad surfaces of our souls. More importantly, our strength came in our ability to be quite flexible. Perhaps we were made of liquid iron? I don't know. What I do know is that this was a mere bank of that iron river, and we were flowing on. But first, a New York slice.

The next few months were jam packed with research about various adoption agencies. We had to take a long, hard look at our "blemishes." T had been involved in some shenanigans when he was younger; could that derail our parenting efforts? According to some agencies, yes. More riverbanks.

I sent emails, I wrote letters, I called many agencies to find out where we belonged. Some of my infertility triggers surfaced, but remember, I was living life to its fullest. Our journey to parenthood was only a small part of our lives, and I was moving along life's path with nary a concern. At least not a concern that would strike me down. I was being the bamboo.

At this point, I was sending every agency a list of all our transgressions in the hopes that someone would say "Well, that's not a big deal" and invite us into their program. We weren't even hinging our hopes on a particular country at that point. Nobody had invited us in, yet I knew an invite was on its way. I simply knew. I trusted. Too much of infertility had been me trusting outside sources (even if they were brilliant docs), and trusting myself felt incredibly empowering. I had no plans to let that go.

One bright, sunny day in August, I was at a doctor's office (not for fertility-related issues for once!), when I got a call from an unknown number. It was local, so I decided to answer it. The voice on the other end introduced herself as the branch director of Holt International, an agency I'd emailed over a month earlier. Because I hadn't heard back from them, I'd written them off completely, so I was surprised when the director called to discuss my email. She carefully went over all the supposed blemishes I'd written about; I told her we'd previously been told we wouldn't qualify to adopt from Korea due to these issues. Her response was glorious: "Every adoption agency is different and has different guidelines, and these are not an issue for us at all. We can absolutely make it work." I was practically floating in air! We'd been invited in! Even though I knew that a call like this was on its way, I was shocked that it was actually happening.

We talked for a few minutes about the process and next steps we should consider taking when she stopped talking suddenly and said, "I'm—I'm so sorry, this is very unprofessional, but my whole office building is shaking!" I was perplexed by this until—sitting in my car in the parking lot of the medical office—my car began to move back and forth! A few car alarms went off. Right at that juncture of our conversation, a 5.8 earthquake had hit New Jersey.

Coming from California and living right near a fault, I never expected an earthquake to hit New Jersey. Neither did she.

Now, one might be a wee bit freaked out that something as rare as an earthquake would happen at the exact moment when I was talking about our next steps to parenthood. I took it as a synchronistic moment—a glorious sign that we were 100% on the right track. We were going to be parents. I told everyone about that experience, and I got laughed at. You might be laughing at me now. But to this day, I maintain the sanctity of that experience. I feel that the Universe literally shook the earth to let me know, "This is it, Maria. It's finally your turn."

After this beautiful phone call that was to be the beginning of our journey with Holt, the stacks of paperwork were like wet noodles smacking me in the face. It sucked. I'd rather study for all the tests I ever took than do that paperwork again. I'd rather do my dissertation—scratch that. Oh hell naw.

Let's be real, writing down all the things that make you you is exceedingly tedious. For instance, we each had to write down the address of every place we'd ever lived. When I found myself at the tenth address, I began to think my family and I were nomads roaming the earth all our lives and I'd never known it. Holy cow! How had we moved so much? T, on the other hand, had had a mere three addresses.

Let's be real again: When it comes to fertility treatment, most of the onus is on the female to get shit done. In my case, it was precisely the same with adoption. The likelihood that I simply took over and didn't delegate is extremely high. I want to call T a butthead for letting me do it, but the fact is, I tend to take over. I annoy myself.

Anyway, after the mile-high load of paperwork was signed, sealed, and delivered, we waited anxiously for any news on movement toward our baby. By December, just before our Christmas trip to Lake Tahoe, we got a phone call saying that our efforts had paid off: we were approved to adopt! Not only were we approved to adopt, but we were approved to adopt from Korea! We were absolutely elated and couldn't wait to announce it to our family. We celebrated like crazy during that holiday season, a season that for the past six years had been incredibly painful for us. We were finally finding some joy in celebrating the holidays again.

At one point, I painstakingly created a video to announce our intent to adopt. I planned to email it to our friends and family and then post it on

Facebook. I still remember my nervous, shaking hand when it was all created and all I had to do was hit "send." I knew we were on a beautiful path, but that path included divulging the very real, dark struggle in not being able to get pregnant. Our struggle would be revealed, and that felt incredible scary.

I felt the fear. And I did it anyway.

The feedback we received was like a roar from a football stadium. I recall tearfully accepting congratulations, hugs from afar, and all manner of positive thoughts and joy from our friends and family. It felt amazing. Many people addressed the infertility in a wonderfully understanding way. They didn't shame me, nor did they try to fix it. Not one person—to my utter shock—said anything about "just" adopting. It was perfect.

At this point, I began to immerse myself into the beautiful Korean culture. I wanted to know everything, and I could not be satiated. I wanted to eat Korean food, see Korean people, speak the Korean language, be in Korea. I wanted to know it all. There was many an evening when T would shake his head and giggle at me as I sat transfixed by Korean soap operas (called K-dramas). I was hooked! I loved this culture so much, even though I'd never been to the country.

Several months after we were approved for the Korean program, we got a phone call from the agency that rocked my world. I wrote a blog post that day that sums up the nuance of emotions quite well:

> You know when you're plugging along, smiling, enjoying life, on a great path toward more happiness, then someone sneaks up behind you and rips the rug right out from under your feet?
>
> You're now sprawled out on the floor, your body trembling, your mind confused, and tears streaming down your face.
>
> This was me the other day.
>
> It all started with a phone call from M at our agency. "Hi, Maria," she said. I could tell after she cleared her throat about five times that something wasn't right.
>
> She then said, "This isn't going to be an easy conversation, so take a deep breath, and I'll get started."
>
> Naturally, I held my breath.
>
> I sat listening for about twenty minutes. Her words were kind of floating around me, and I thought I understood them but then felt as if I were in some kind of dream world. Could this really be happening? No way, man. We've finally escaped the grips of infertility! We're on this very solid path to adoption, and we couldn't be happier! What is she talking about???

You all know that things with the Korean program have been winding down, making the process slower and slower. We were prepared to deal with that.

Recently, we received what we thought was good news: In August, the finalization of adoptions will take place in Korea at court while parents are still there with their babies. It used to be that parents had to come back to the U.S., and the baby wasn't officially theirs until the process finished up here in the U.S. (some families are still on that track). The premise of this new policy is that it gives Korea more control over who adopts their babies. Fair enough.

A couple of days ago, our agency found out another caveat in the process, which I'm unable to share publicly, per the agency. It basically means that T and I have to put our adoption process on hold for about a year (maybe less). At that time, we can either move forward or we'll have to switch programs. We won't know. Here we thought we were on a clear track to bring home our baby (finally!) by this time or maybe a little later next year; then this.

Buh-bye, rug.

We were given the option of switching programs now. We can go with China's Child of Promise program, which is actually a little scary for us. We have to be open to more possible health issues with the baby, and that makes us uncomfortable. Further, China doesn't have an excellent foster care system like Korea does, and I worry about attachment issues.

The positives of China: 1) It's about $5,000 less expensive (since we're not paying into a foster care system), 2) We can have a baby by February or March 2013, and 3) I can't think of anything more at this point. I'm still too attached to Korea.

I'm also afraid to get too attached to China. What if someone takes my rug again?

This whole process is also triggering a lot of infertility emotions. This is exactly what it's like, albeit in shorter segments: Hope, loss, hope, loss, hope, loss…the cycle doesn't end.

Right now, T and I are in discussion mode. I've got a call in to an International Adoption Center at a pediatrician's office to get more education on some of these health issues. We're hoping that will make us feel better about switching.

I despise this unsettled feeling.

Unsettled, indeed. That phone call triggered many infertility memories, and at one point I found myself curled up in the fetal position, crying and snotty again, unsure of what to do next. Like being kicked to the curb by my former friend, I was experiencing a storm of emotions. Here was the difference: When

I was stuck in infertility mind, I'd get lost in fetal-position mode. The haze of depression would linger for days, weeks, or longer. I'd let a phone call like this—granted, a big one— grab hold of my psyche and take over my life, and I wouldn't let it go. It was like following the storm wherever it went rather than letting it do its thing and glide past me. I would let it color every single nuance of my life as if the only thing that mattered in the world was that I'd gotten some shitty news.

Being solidly different now—being the bamboo—I was able to allow the wave of sadness to wash over me. I invited it in like a familiar, albeit scratchy, sweater, and I let it hang out for a while. Then, when the intensity of the moment passed, I was able to put the sweater back on the closet shelf and move on with my life. I was the bamboo tree, taken down for a minute with my flexibility, but I was able to recover my genuine zest for life and move on to next steps with nary a scratch. I was honestly floored by my ability to do that. Even though I'd worked on it for so long, I was in awe of the ease with which I floated above the sadness, observed it with kindness and compassion, and carried on once the wave had passed.

> **I floated above the sadness, observed it with kindness and compassion, and carried on once the wave had passed.**

The agency suggested we speak with another family who was already in the China program, and in the end, we found ourselves agreeing to switch. Where our child came from mattered much less to us than when our child came to us. We were ready right now, and China was a sure bet. The following weeks were a blur of more paperwork, as we had to add three times more info to a dossier for China, and I distracted myself with that.

All the while, I had an intuition—a nagging sensation hanging out in the back of my mind and in my heart. The entire time I was completing new paperwork for China, I knew that our baby was in Korea.

Fertility Key: Be the Bamboo (aka Be Okay with What Is)

There's a freedom in knowing we can survive peacefully during chaos. There's empowerment in knowing we have a choice in how we're going to react to stressful situations. In every single interaction in your daily life, you have a choice: Am I going to live a What-IF life, or am I going to live a What-IS life? Stay with me because these acronyms are important.

Let's start with IF. We know this one, right? It stands for infertility, and I mentioned way back in the beginning of this book that it's also that realm of possibility we so fervently wonder about. What happens if…? What if…? At the core, attending to this acronym keeps us out of the present moment, focused on a future we can't grasp yet or the past we'd like to leave behind (e.g., What if I hadn't taken birth control pills? Drank too much? Placed my child for adoption? Said that mean thing?).

How about the acronym IS? I like to think of IS as the acronym for inspiration. Take a look at the word *inspiration*—it's the combination of two words: *in* and *spirit*. When you're living an inspired life, you're living from a spiritual place. I referred to IS in the last chapter when talking about how to trust your inner guide—your intuition—to lead you in a healthy direction. When you live from an inspired place, your inner guide is never far away, and it's always whispering gently what your next moves are. In direct contrast to IF, IS keeps you firmly in the present. When you're living from a place of inspiration, you silence the chaos right now so you can "hear" what your intuition is gently whispering. Not only am I talking about living an inspired life, I'm talking about living your inspired life in the present moment. Even when it sucks.

Obviously, living an inspired life when everything is going our way is easy, isn't it? We can skip along, loving exactly how life is while dreaming of our future endeavors or past successes. But when infertility hits, we're promptly derailed. The following practices are designed to help you handle hard shit.

Straight up. All the previous chapters have been building your strengths for handling the difficulties that come your way; below are practices to help you move through those difficult moments with as few bumps as possible. Please don't expect an absence of bumps. There will be plenty of them, large and small, like when I heard the news of having to switch adoption programs. Like me, you may even find yourself in the fetal position on the floor somewhere. The difference will be that you'll observe the bumps, accept the bumps, and move over them with less suffering, more ease, and more grace. The points is, you'll be okay with what's happening right then and there, accepting it even when it sucks. In time, you'll learn to love whatever comes your way, seeing hard experiences as opportunities for growth. For now, it's okay to just be okay with hard stuff. The rest will come in time.

Action Steps: Living from What IS Rather Than What IF

You've done a ton of work thus far. I'd like to offer a pause to honor how awesome you are for taking care of yourself in this way.

...

...

...

I'd also like you to write "Nicely done, Beautiful" on a sticky note and put it where you'll see these words every day. You deserve it!

And now to move into more work…

The exercises below are geared toward helping you live your IS life rather than an IF life. This is just the start of moving toward total present-moment awareness and seeing the beauty in everything—even the hard stuff. For now, we're focusing on what to do with hard feelings and how to use words to change our energetic experience of feelings. "Energetic experience?" you ask? I'll explain more in a bit. For now, "Feelings, nothing more than feelings…"

Exercise 1: Feelings Blow. Feel Them Anyway.

Feelings suck. Well, the hard ones at least. And we spend a lot of time attempting to run away from them. As any therapist will tell you, much of the work we do is around creating an open space for people to just feel their feelings. We slow people down, refraining from fixing anything, so they can simply feel what's coming up. That's why therapy feels terrible sometimes. I've been a therapy client, too, and I know the experience of being in a room with all eyes on me just feeling my immensely painful feelings. Snot and tissue are typically present as well.

The thing is, if you've dealt with infertility, you've proven you can do hard things. You've also proven you can survive without having all the answers. You may have experienced ignoring your hard feelings, which only serves to make them lie in wait. They will pop up again to hound you. Trust me. It's much healthier (and more efficient!) to feel the feelings. You can feel your hard feelings without needing to "fix" them, without needing to feel better immediately, and without having to stuff them down and act as if all is well. The fact is, your feelings are incredible guides. Just like you trust your body to give you pain when something isn't right, your emotions do the same for your psyche and spirit. Feeling all your emotions does not mean weakness. Think about it: Feeling all that pain is not for the weak!

Get out your journal for this exercise, please. Write down the word FEEL in a column like this:

F

E

E

L

Each time you have difficult feelings, head on over to this exercise.

F: Feel your feelings. Ask yourself, What feelings am I having? Name them. What do those feelings feel like in my body? Beating heart? Heaviness? Fast breath? A headache? Name the sensations.

E: Empathy. Give yourself some empathy, self-compassion. Give yourself permission to feel what you're feeling. No beating yourself up. Write,

"It's okay that I'm feeling _____." Then ask yourself, "How are these feelings guiding me?" Write what first comes to mind.

E: Emote. Here's where you really let the feelings go. Cry, run, hike, meditate, journal, go for a bike ride—whatever you need to do to really manifest those feelings on the outside. This is the equivalent of taking off your infertility mask and really letting the real you shine through. Write down what you did and how helpful it was. If it was helpful, you can use it again next time; if not, now you know to try something else.

L: Let it go. Once you've done the above exercises, check in with yourself. On a scale of 1–10, how intense are these feelings? If they're a 3 or below, you're ready to let them go. If not, they require more processing, and that takes you back to the empathy step. Letting feelings go can be a simple thought, or it can be a physical representation of letting go. I personally like journaling goodbye to my feelings and closing the book. It's like a period at the end of a sentence. Done. Find what works for you to let them go. When you feel more peaceful—though not necessarily 100% peaceful—you'll know you've begun to let go. Keep in mind, letting go often requires more than a second. Sometimes it takes a few days. Be patient, loving, and kind with yourself.

Exercise 2: Words Matter

There's some tremendous research done by Dr. Masaru Emoto about the power of words. In his *New York Times* bestseller, *The Hidden Messages of Water*, Dr. Emoto outlines experiments involving water crystals and how words affect them. The experiments indicated positive words producing symmetrical and aesthetically pleasing ice crystals, whereas negative words produced asymmetrical and "ugly" ice crystals. Dr. Emoto suggested that the energy behind the words had a physical effect on the water molecules. The idea is, if our words can affect water in this way and our bodies are made up of mostly water, imagine what our words do to our bodies.

I firmly believe that creating positive change is affected by the words we use. However, I posit that change involves more than the actual words themselves; the intent behind the words is where the power lies. Here's an example: I once had a roommate who named her cat "Shithead." Shithead was a beautiful black-and-white domestic long-haired kitty, and she was loved immensely. Her name was simply a term of endearment, and it was said with that particular intent. Now, back in my everything-sucks-due-to-infertility days, I would call someone a shithead on the NJ highway, and it was certainly not a term of endearment. There was vehemence behind that term. And if that person heard me screeching that name at them, they would have a physical response, wouldn't they? I definitely had a physical response by using that word and having that intent. See what I mean? Words matter, and the intent behind them matters, too.

There's an absolute energetic response with the words we use. This is a big part of "stop kicking the puppy" from chapter six. Now that you've stopped using words to harm yourself, I'm asking you to change the intention behind how you treat yourself as well. This skill is essential in being the bamboo. You begin to allow the feelings to move through you without judging yourself or anyone else along the way. It's a shortcut to the "other side" of hard emotions.

This is another journal exercise. Please take out your journal and draw a line down the center of a blank page. On the first side, write, "Negative Words/Intent," and on the second side write, "Positive Words/Intent."

Now I want you to get nasty. Think of a situation that really upsets you. Write every little negative thing you can think of about infertility, a person, your job, your partner, your neighbor, your car, etc., in the first column. Write as many things as you can without stopping. The point in this part of the exercise is to really let your rude, mean self fly. If it's hard to write anything, consider these questions: What emotions do you have? What thoughts do you have? What do you wish were different about this?

When you've come up with a list of ten or more, stop. Now, at the end of this list, write "Body Sensations" and list how your body feels. You may notice tense shoulders, a tight jaw, halted breath, a scowl, a headache. I once worked with someone who said she felt stress between her knees and her feet. It doesn't matter where you notice the sensations, just notice them. Tensing up the body in any way is a state of stress. Even without Dr. Emoto's research, you can tell that negative words and intents have a direct impact on your body.

Now I want you to get pleasant. Think of a situation that brings you joy or pleasure. This could be a memory, a future endeavor, or something happening in your world right now. It should bring a little twinkle to your eye. Write down every little thing about this situation. What emotions do you have? What thoughts do you have? What is amazing about this experience? When you have a list of ten or more items, stop. Just like in the previous column, write, "Body

Sensations" at the bottom of the list and write what you now notice about your body. Is your scowl gone? Have your shoulders relaxed? Is your jaw more slack? Maybe you've let your stomach out?

Now that you know how your body responds to positive and negative words, how will you choose to talk about your fertility journey? Write it all down on a fresh page in your journal. Remember, you're looking for intention. So writing something negative is not necessarily a terrible thing. For example, "This journey has been difficult; I am so much stronger than I thought I was." This sentence starts out acknowledging the pain, and the ultimate intention behind it is positive.

> **Now that you know how your body responds to positive and negative words, how will you choose to talk about your fertility journey?**

Here's another cool thing about this exercise: Whenever you notice that your body is having a reaction, you'll be able to recognize you're having an emotion tied to it. I can't tell you how many times I've noticed that my shoulders are tense on a drive home and I'm able to address it right there by physically changing my body and mentally changing the imagery or words I'm thinking. If you're dealing with infertility, I know that you already have a phenomenal sense of your body. Listen to it; it'll never steer you wrong.

Fertility Mantra

Practice this mantra in the morning and in the evening for the next ten days.

Breathing in: Feelings are hard.

Breathing out: I am feeling them anyway.

Breathing in: This journey is hard.

Breathing out: I've proven I can do hard things

(Repeat three times.)

Fertility Meditation: A Memory Ride

Do this meditation daily for the next ten days. (Reminder: You can access my recordings of this and all other meditations from this book at www.drmariarothenburger.com/transcendingmeditations.)

This meditation is designed to help you become the observer of your experience rather than being engulfed in intense emotion. The goal is for you to be open to the experience of everything and attached to nothing.

Begin by making yourself comfortable in whatever position feels best to you. Lying down or sitting in an upright position. Back straight but not stiff. Place your hands in a comfortable position, perhaps in your lap or lying along your side.

Take three deep breaths through your nose and exhale through your mouth.

Inhale…

Exhale…

[Long pause]

Allow your breathing to return to normal now. Whatever rhythm your body natural produces is perfectly fine and healthy.

We are going to go on a memory ride. All the while, know that you are safe, and that this level of relaxation is completely healthy for you. If you need to at any time, simply open your eyes and you will be back in your current space.

Now, take a moment to reflect on yourself one year younger. Think about where you were one year ago, what you were doing, who you were surrounded by…everything about you one year ago.

[Long pause]

Now, reflect back to the you from five years ago. First think about what year that was. Who were you then? What kind of clothing did you wear? Did you work? Go to school? What people were important to you in your life then? What endeavors were important to you?

[Long pause]

Think about a time now when you were a teenager Who were your friends? What was school like for you? What did you do for fun? Who was important to you then?

[Long pause]

Leaving those years, you are now heading into pre-teen years Physically see yourself at that age before your eyes. What are you wearing? Who is with you? Who and what are the important people and things to you at this age?

[Long pause]

And now, leaving your pre-teen years, allow your mind to drift back further to age ten and younger. We are going to stay here for a little while. Imagine yourself now in school at that age. I'd like you now to think about a time in school that was particularly challenging. Whatever memory first pops up is the right one. Stay with that. Imagine yourself now in that difficult time.

[Long pause]

What about this memory is hard? What emotions do you recall having? See yourself as if you are watching a movie. What would you like to say to the character that is you in this scenario? Is there anything you'd like to do for this little kid?

And now, consider out of the thousands of memories you could have pulled up from your memory bank, why this one? What about this memory can be applied to your current adult life? Would the things you would say to yourself as a kid apply now?

Feel whatever feelings come up, knowing you are safe, knowing you are wiser for having completed this exercise.

And now watch the memory fade away. You're slowly moving into middle school, high school…and now five years ago, now one year ago.

You are now once again in the present moment. Notice what your body is resting on. Wiggle your toes and fingers. Take a deep breath. Flutter your eyes open.

What's Next?

Living fully in the present moment, awaiting the next storm, moving through it with ease, finding beauty in everything around you, feeling all your feelings…geez, you're doing some awesome work! You're now ready to create miracles. The next chapter asks you to get into that headspace, heartspace, and energetic field of possibility. In direct contrast to the negative and scary "what if" thinking inherent in infertility, you're ready to begin thinking, "What if miracles happen? What if my baby is on his/her way? What if this is my time? What if I've created a space for my baby to come safely? What if the next cycle is it? What if this time next year I have my baby in my arms?" This is all within the realm of positive possibility. The next chapter is about creating that positive, intentional space for yourself. In effect, you'll be co-creating your future reality.

Chapter Nine

What If Miracles Happen?

I am realistic. I expect miracles.
– Dr. Wayne Dyer

This is the chapter where shit gets real. There isn't another way to put it. Everything you've read thus far will come to fruition in this chapter in ways that seem absolutely magical.

Every. Single. Word. Is. True.

Upon researching this chapter, I often gazed, eyes wide open, at the pages of my blog that documented every action and reaction. I understand if you don't believe it. I still don't believe that it happened, and I lived it!

This chapter is the culmination of all the lessons you've learned thus far. The importance of getting into the headspace of miracles happening cannot be stressed enough. You've begun to remove a ton of negativity from your life, including healing pain and noticing how you've changed because of painful experiences. You've honored your pain by giving it your attention. Now you're ready for the part where you create miracles.

Before we move on with this chapter, I'd like to ask you to consider one thing. If you catch yourself thinking, "Yeah, but that's *her* story; that could never happen to me," redirect yourself for even a moment, and think, "Huh, I wonder what it would feel like if a miracle happened for me?" And then feel it. Feel every glorious sensation. Feel the smile form on your mouth, the tears come to your eyes, and the gratitude explode in your heart. Everything I, my clients, and my fertility-challenged friends have experienced, you can have too. In fact, it's already on its way.

At this point, I've gotten vulnerable, taken off my infertility mask, embraced my imperfection, stopped shoulding all over myself, made my whole life important—not just infertility— trusted my gut, let go of the outcome, and trusted the process. Everything in me pointed to the moments you are about to read about. I've become a lover of meditation, gardening, my work, and being with my animals and husband. I find joy in the little things—and I do mean little, like the way a breeze cools my skin. I still get sad; I still get triggered. But I know what to do with that now. I don't resist the infertility wind; I'm the flexible bamboo. But before I say goodbye to the storm of sadness, I give it a little hug. I say, "I love you, and you're okay. You were always okay." This line of thinking and being is hopefully where you're headed as well as you complete the action steps in this book.

The following story is a miracle. It's a host of miracles, truth be told, and I'm still in awe. I am so looking forward to the day when you get to be in awe of your own miracles, too.

Fertility Friends in the White City

There are two beautiful women in my life whom I've come to consider two of my very best friends. K, C, and I met online. Fortunately for me—just like T—they were not axe murderers. These ladies were just the balance of fortitude and hippie-ish thinking I loved being around. We met in an infertility forum all about alternative ways of getting pregnant. Even before we met in person, we felt closer than others who see each other every day.

The three of us began our fertility journeys right around the same time, and we were solidly in the thick of it when we met. Because we were so like-minded and needed some serious girl time away from the world, we decided to get together in person—three internet friends meeting for the first time yet already knowing the depths of one another's hearts in a way that takes years for most in-person friends to experience.

We met in Chicago's beautiful White City (I will never forget how clean it is!) and promptly got busy having some girl fun. K, with her pragmatic skill, escorted C and I all around her beloved city, which she knew like the back of her hand. We enjoyed gorgeous sites, delicious food (deep dish anyone?), architecture that left my mouth agape, museums, park strolls, and lovely shared stories.

During that first visit, I kept myself a wee bit distant. T and I were having a very difficult time in our marriage at the time, and I wasn't yet ready to divulge that intense bit of news. I just wanted to escape my everyday life. K and C were the perfect remedy. They, I'm sure, sensed my disconnection at times, and they embraced me anyway. I loved them almost instantly.

There are few who truly understand the path of the infertile. I recall having to explain myself to a couple of therapists before I grew too exasperated to even see them anymore. With K and C, I could make a quiet comment or give a certain facial expression and be instantly understood. They were the breath of fresh air I desperately needed during this life crisis.

I recall the day I shakily picked up the phone to have a three-way conversation with them. I wanted to tell them one of my darkest secrets: T and I were not well. I was dipping my toe into vulnerability, and it scared the shit out of me. Even with these two women whom I trusted immensely, I was terrified to let them into my dark world. At the time, I was still wearing my infertility mask quite well, and there were few, if any, people who knew how much I was dying inside.

So although K and C wholeheartedly agreed to talk with me, I almost backed out. ("I have something very important to talk with you guys about. Can we chat? Yes? Shit.") But I didn't back out. I lay on my bed, nausea enveloping me as I divulged the most difficult part of my life to them. T and I were looking divorce square in the face.

And they gave me a virtual hug.

They did not pity me. They did not tell me I could do better anyway. They did not offer pithy words of advice. They did not say a single word that would raise my defensive ire. Rather, every word they offered was like hot cocoa and a fire after a particularly frigid hike through a blizzard. I knew right then, these were friends for life. How could I be so raw, so open, so trusting with them and not keep them around forever? Sorry, K and C, you're stuck with me.

I don't recall the words I used or even how that conversation ended. I just know I felt lighter and freer after inviting K and C into my darkness. Somehow that single conversation shined a little light somewhere. And I knew I'd be okay.

A couple of years later—after T and I had done immense marriage work and were on the healing track—K, C, and I were all solidly still on the family-growing track. After many heartbreaking failed cycles, the three of us finally felt movement in our journeys. K had successfully completed a donor IVF cycle and was pregnant with twins. C had successfully completed an IVF cycle and was pregnant with a singleton. They were due very close to each other the following summer. I had moved on to the adoption track and was looking to have my baby in my arms likely a year after they had theirs.

A word about envy: One might think that after years of infertility, these two pregnancies would fill me with envy. But I can honestly say (and I looked back at my journals to hold myself accountable) there was absolutely zero envy when it came to K's and C's pregnancies. I was as happy for them as I would have been for myself, and I was not sad at all about my not being pregnant. I think this is a complicated matter, though, so I shall riff on it for a bit.

There are several factors that I propose led to my non-envy when it should have been a-blazin'. First, I had stopped shoulding on myself long ago. Second, I'd never been particularly interested in pregnancy per se; for me, it was a means to an end. Third, I was so damn grateful for every little thing in my life at that point, I had no room for envy in any area. Fourth, and most importantly, K and C were (and are) dear friends of mine who'd suffered greatly through their own journeys. I wish I could tell you their stories now—they're riveting, sorrowful, and filled with boundless joy. Alas, they own their stories, which I encourage them to wear with pride. We all have our battle scars. And together, there is no envy—only great, great love, admiration, and respect for all we went through to have our babies in our arms. Envy doesn't belong in that space.

Why do I bring this up here? Because little did I know the incredible miracle that was about to happen for all three of us. I don't know the odds of this happening, but all these years later, we still speak of it with absolute awe. Let's continue with the rest of our journey, shall we?

317

If you'll recall where we left off on the path to adoption, T and I had switched to the China program. At this point, I was heavily practiced at listening to my intuition. I looked all over the place for signs that I was on the right track. I was getting very good at listening to the nuances of my body and feelings, looking outward, and being quite curious about the answers coming my way. I saw synchronicities all over the place. "Hey!" I might say, "I was literally just thinking of a hummingbird, and there one is!"

Over the last year or so, I kept seeing the numbers 3, 1, and 7 all over the place. I would see them on license plates, football scores, gas prices. There were endless places they would keep showing up. I even laughingly pulled them out of a fortune cookie once. I had no real idea why those numbers kept showing up, and I was not into numerology or anything remotely similar; I only knew they were significant to me, because T's birthday is March 17. It's a giant celebration on the East Coast where everyone celebrates St. Patrick's Day along with T. There's an abundance of corned beef and cabbage, and most everyone dons something green. When I moved to the East Coast, I could no longer get away with claiming I was safe because I had green eyes. I had to wear green, or else.

One day T suggested I play the lottery, since I kept referencing seeing 3, 1, and 7 everywhere. I laughed. I'd never played the lottery before, but when the opportunity to get a ticket presented itself, I took it. We were at a Christmas party at the neighbor's house, and we were playing a white elephant game. (If you don't know what that is, Google it. It's super fun!) There were three sets of lottery tickets going around the room, and there was one set that had more trades left, so when my turn came up, I "stole" those lottery tickets from someone, thinking "why not?"

The next morning when T was in the kitchen brewing coffee, I decided to scratch off my lottery tickets. There were a couple of tickets with a few dollars' worth of winnings. Score! I giggled to myself that this had to be what 3, 1, 7 meant. I scratched off the final lottery ticket. I looked at the results, looked at the rules of the game, looked back at the results, looked back at the rules. Then I said loud enough for T to hear me in the kitchen, "Hun? I think I just won $5,000."

"Get outta heah," came the reply in a thick New Jersey accent.

"No really. I think I won five grand on this lottery ticket." He came into the room.

"Lemme see dat." He looked at the results, read the rules, looked at the results, read the rules, and said, "Holy shit, I think you just won $5,000." After a few minutes of laughing uncontrollably and dancing around in the living room, I read how to claim my prize. Only then did I notice the name of the specific game printed on the ticket: "Happy Birthday." March 17 was important after all!

I was living off my intuition now. No matter what, I knew I could pay attention to my gut. So many other things went my way without having to think through the steps, I began to trust that all would be well no matter what avenue I took. I learned to pay attention to every feeling that came my way, even if everything in my world pointed to the opposite being the truth. It was like looking at the resume of someone and seeing how great they looked on paper, but when you meet them there's just something that isn't quite right. When I have the "isn't quite right" feeling, I get curious about it and typically pause before making a decision. On the other hand, if there are blemishes on paper but my gut feeling is one of complete and total ease, I typically move toward the sensation of total ease. As such, I went through my days following through with the required adoption documentation for the China program, yet I had an inkling—a knowing—that our baby was in Korea. I can't explain it other than to say it was a strong intuition. It felt easy, it felt calm, and I knew I simply had to pay attention to whatever was in my path to let me know that was where we were headed.

I recall one particularly pensive—now incredibly significant—morning on my way to the office, when I looked squarely at a sign with the Korean alphabet (Hangul) on it. It was a sign for a Korean church I must have passed several hundred times. I believe I knew there was a church on the corner, but I only now recognized the Hangul since I had been learning all about Korea for many months. As I passed by the sign, I felt as if I were in a dream. Next to the sign was a mailbox with the street numbers painted in white: 317.

After I picked my jaw up off the floor, I took this as an absolute sign from the Universe that our baby was on the way from Korea. I didn't know how that was to happen, but I knew that I was to trust it. I was to trust that miracles happen and I need not do a thing but be open and wait. And I did. I had total faith that the Universe had our back; we need only be grateful and open to the gifts that were to come.

One month later, on a gorgeous spring day in May, the gift came. Below is what I wrote in my blog on that unforgettable day.

We Interrupt This Zen Moment

…to bring you earth-shattering, life-altering news.

In a good way.

That's basically what I heard yesterday after having received a phone call from our agency's director during my hike with the dogs. I usually take them hiking once a week to let them run free and to commune with nature. It's totally zen, and I love it.

So, I'm walking along listening to birds chirp and watching the dogs be in the moment when the ring of my phone marred those lovely sounds of nature. I bring my phone with me as a just-in-case kinda thing because I got lost hiking once (thankfully, my dog got me outta there…animals are awesome).

I didn't recognize the number, so I didn't answer it and was actually surprised to hear the familiar ping letting me know there was a voicemail. I picked it up.

And that's when my zen was entirely disrupted.

The director said something to the effect of, "We have an urgent situation, and I need you to call me as soon as possible."

"Shit," is what I thought. "What else? Now we're not eligible for China either???"

Obviously I called back immediately. She asked if I was sitting. I told her I was hiking, but I'd find a rock. And I did. She then proceeded to tell me the craziest thing ever: A family just had their adopted son escorted from Korea last Friday, and they aren't doing well. For privacy reasons, I won't go into detail, but basically, they don't want to finalize the adoption.

And our agency is asking us to adopt him!!!!!!

We have to decide by today, and he would need to be placed with us by Friday.

Yeah. Thank God I was sitting.

We're scared shitless, and nervous, and feeling crazy, and overwhelmed. We have nothing. No car seat, no toddler food, no toys, no bath stuff, no nursery set-up, no outlet covers. Nothing. Zip. Zilch. Nada.

But we have love. We have a LOT of love.

Come to think of it, the whole scared-nervous-crazy-overwhelmed thing? Um, that sounds a lot like we're preparing for another IVF. We know how to do that!

Are you up for a wild ride? I think we are.

Now it's your turn to pick up your jaw from the floor. I'll wait.

I am assuming you caught the part about this little boy having been born in Korea. Suddenly the $5,000 lottery ticket is like chump change. Am I right? As much as I wholeheartedly trusted that the Universe provides and we need only wait for the gifts, this bit of news absolutely blew my mind. I'm pretty sure I ended the call a blabbering mess, somehow conveying I should probably run it by T first, but every part of me was screaming, "YES! YES, we want this baby! It isn't even a question!"

T wasn't living in my zen space. He brought me right back down to earth with all his stupidly practical questions like, "How can we do this? We have no help, we didn't give clients/work notice, we don't have anything for a baby, we don't even have a space for him to sleep in!" Well damn. Buh-bye wind in my sails. He was right. And for a good few hours, I felt terrified. I'd let my mind wander back along with T's to the space of needing to control the Universe. I needed to have ducks in a row, and I needed to know how every step was going to go along the way. After a few hours of that, I realized I'd traveled right back to where my brain had been completely unsuccessful for many years. In short, I was being an idiot.

I began to collaborate with T on the possibility of saying yes to this adoption opportunity, knowing full well this was our son. There was no doubt in my mind. But T's mind didn't work like mine, and we were a team. Once I realized I was being an idiot, I simply stayed there with T while his brain processed this hugely miraculous news. And process he did. It's kind of funny to me now how he accepted the $5,000 lottery win much faster. At the end of all the processing, and with a few hours to spare, we called the agency and told them we were freaked the fuck out and…we couldn't wait to meet our son.

I'd been carefully chronicling our journey in my blog called *From IF to When*, and I couldn't wait to announce the long-awaited arrival of our family member number three. It was an astounding and miraculous experience, and we'll never forget a second of it. Still, it's fun to read through the details. Here's that post:

> At 11:48am on May 25, 2012 our lives changed forever. 8 months, 2 weeks, and 3 days since applying to adopt.
>
> After we waited with bated breath for the bank to open, got some documents notarized, emailed them to the agency's director, and did some

last-minute shopping, we got the phone call from the social worker that she would be arriving in 45 minutes.

Our hearts stopped. Could this really be happening? Like seriously?

When the social worker showed up, I frantically tried to put the battery back in the camera, so we could get some shots, and T was outside cleaning off the porch yelling, "They're here! Maria, they're here!!!"

My neighbor happened to be outside when they drove up, saw him, and started crying. We've been waiting so long for this (She went through infertility as well and had twins via IVF), and she knows all about our story.

Then T and I saw him.

An absolute angel.

And we knew he was ours.

The social worker carried him into the house while her friend snapped like a billion photos. She sat on the couch and chatted with us on either side to help him get acclimated. Naturally, we wanted to hold him, and kiss him, and squeeze those ridiculously cute cheeks immediately! But, of course, for his sweet sake, we held back. Eventually, we made our way to the floor where he couldn't resist the Mega Bloks we had gotten him. The social worker sneaked out from behind him, and voila! Family of three; playing on the living room floor. As if that's how it always was.

He didn't cry once. It was more like he was curious and, of course, confused. But he had no trouble checking things out.

After two hours of hanging with us, he was laughing up a storm, showing us his ridiculously adorable smile, complete with gigantic dimple. The social worker called, our adoption social worker called, and the director called just to check in with us. He was babbling in the background and totally making us laugh with his antics.

He belongs with us. There's no doubt in our minds. Yesterday he started calling T "Oppa," which is Daddy in Korean. Today, it was clear he's calling me "Umma." He's seemingly very attached to us already, loves holding our hands, and loves gazing into our eyes. He's a love muffin.

There are some things we have to work through....like he does NOT like naps. At all. He doesn't like bathtime. At all. And he doesn't like the stroller. At all. Well...the big stroller. He was fine in the umbrella stroller where he fell asleep on a walk today. From what I read, sponge baths are normal in Korea, so he's probably not used to a bathtub. We'll just continue to do whatever he's used to for a while and slllloooowwlllly get him into doing new things.

It's sometimes difficult to understand what our little Bub has been through. We have to be gentle and follow his lead. We want to show him off to the world. We've wanted this for SO. LONG. and holding back on throwing a Welcome Home party is difficult. But it's no sacrifice when we think of his well-being. Anything he wants at this point.

Except my iPhone, which he keeps wanting to play with. I'm pretty sure he didn't get to play with an iPhone in Korea either. lol.

To that end, I'm so grateful. So, so grateful to Bub's birthparents, foster parents, and even the family here in the U.S. who decided not to keep him. No judgment. Just immense gratitude for all of them for bringing our little man to us.

THIS is what we've been waiting for. This is our "When."

Sigh. Even now I get chills. This alone is a major miracle, and it gives one pause to even accept that something this big could happen. I'm here to tell you that this is entirely possible, and not just because it happened to me. I've seen countless miracles happen, I've stopped being as astounded and have begun living as if that's the way it's supposed to be. And I believe it is. If I needed more evidence to that fact, here's one: Way back in Chapter 2, I made a comment about being obsessed with our kid being a lefty and having dimples. Turns out, our little guy is a lefty and has one giant dimple in his cheek. How's that for evidence?

To add to our miracle, a few weeks after our little man came home to be in our arms forever, K and C got their miracles, too. K's boy-girl twins and C's little boy were born in June, and suddenly we were all on the other side of infertility. We were navigating this weird new world, unsure of our footing yet so grateful to be there. The timing of this is not lost on me. It's not only astonishing that we each got our miracles after many long, arduous years but that we found one another and had our babies within a month of one another is particularly mind blowing. I don't know a soul who could have predicted such synchronicity.

I think it's important to note, just as I did in the above blog post, that having our baby home felt like he'd always been there. I'd thought about this moment for what seemed an eternity, I felt the feelings, I fantasized about the songs I would sing and the walks we would take and the family time we'd have together as a family of three (plus two dogs and two cats). And, unlike the beginning of our journey, I didn't fantasize with a desperate plea to the Universe. I simply lived as if he were already there. This is an extremely important key to creating miracles in your life; if you take away nothing else from this entire book, take this with you. Begin living as if your miracle is already here.

Fertility Key: You Can Create Miracles

Miracles for Your Body

Miracles seem far-fetched, don't they? By definition, they don't come to fruition by any explainable science and are therefore considered to have come from a divine source. I'm saying right now that you are a divine being, and you can therefore create miracles. If you're like me a couple of decades ago, you're rolling your eyes right now thinking, "Aw, man, I was on board until she got all hippie on me." I would still be rolling my eyes if it weren't for the fact that I thought about being a mom through adoption of a little boy in Korea, and several months later, despite all the supposed evidence that it wasn't going to happen, he showed up. That's an undeniable fact. Mind you, this isn't the only time I've let go of control, trusted big things to happen, and had things just show up. Like the time we had no jobs and no place to live, packed up all our shit into a sixteen-foot moving truck, and drove cross-country to start fresh. I just knew that all would be well and that we'd be safe and happy. There were bumps and obstacles, of course, but in the end: jobs, shelter, happiness.

Even though miracles can manifest in all areas your life, let's start with a brief explanation of how this process works for your body. It may seem a little more scientific than you thought. You may be familiar with Dr. Joe Dispenza's work already. If not, hang on to your hats and glasses, because I'm about to get nerdy. Dr. Dispenza is a chiropractor and neuroscientist who speaks in practical terms about how our thoughts affect our bodies. In short, every time we create a thought, our brains send signals to the cells in our bodies via chemicals. So think about this: If our cells are responding to chemical correspondence of thought, then our cells are literally the way they are because of our thoughts. But what is actually changing in our cells, you may ask? Dr. Bruce Lipton, in his book *The Biology of Belief*, talks about chemical signals communicating to our cells what genes need to be expressed based on the signals being received. Put simply, your thoughts change which genes are expressed.

> **If our cells are responding to chemical correspondence of thought, then our cells are literally the way they are because of our thoughts.**

In the fertility world, this is apparent when we live month after month, desperately attempting to create fertility (stressful thoughts), when we keep having thoughts that we're infertile. If instead, you begin thinking "I am fertile," you'll begin sending signals to your body that you are indeed fertile (calm, joyful thoughts).

Here's a real-life example: I have a genetic predisposition to endometriosis, meaning that this condition runs in my family. When I live with stressful thoughts, my brain sends signals to my cells that it's time to express the genes that are in line with stress. For me, that is endometriosis and other health issues. If, however, I quiet the desperation in me and consciously begin to imagine being in the future I want to be in, the messages sent to my cells are those of wellness, and my cells will begin to express the genes that match wellness. Incidentally, I haven't had symptoms of endometriosis since about six months after beginning to practice the concepts in this book.

Miracles Beyond the Body

We've been talking about utilizing your consciousness, thoughts, and emotions to make real changes in your biology. You might be thinking, that's all well and good, but what does this have to do with a little Korean boy showing up on your doorstep? Here's where things get weird and, frankly, controversial. Once again, I encourage you to do your own research. I've done my own over many years, and this is the only way I can explain our son showing up the way he did. Let's start with some science, shall we?

There's a famous experiment in quantum physics called the double-slit experiment. In this experiment, light (or matter) directed at a pair of slits exhibits characteristics of both waves and particles. As *Popular Mechanics* described it, "The logic-defying double-slit experiment is even weirder than you thought." They're right. The results transcend the boundaries of

Newtonian physics, which explains much about our universe and all that's in it: things we can touch and feel and the behaviors of particles. However, as the double-slit experiment suggests, there's a slew of things that occur on the subatomic, quantum level that can't be explained by classical physics. Explaining the entirety of this experiment is beyond the scope of this book, so I'll just get to the two major conclusions:

1. All possibilities exist at the same time.
2. What you attend to is what is made manifest.

Are you fully grasping now how powerful this makes you? It's amazing. Just like the photons shot at the double slits, all possibilities for your future parenthood reality exist at the same time. It's your attention to what you want (e.g., living as if your baby is already here) that creates that reality. What you think about, how you live, and how you perceive things are meaningful. Your whole attitude, how you embody fertility struggles, and how you move through stress and struggle are meaningful. You matter. And you are incredibly powerful. Just sit with that for a minute.

Now, here's something that trips up most people dealing with infertility. If I've heard it once, I've heard it a thousand times: "But Maria, I don't want to set myself up for major disappointment by thinking I already have what I don't actually have. I'd rather prepare myself for the worst." Well, I have news for you, my friend. If you're living in the headspace of what-if-the-worse-thing-happens, you'll be creating the perfect petri dish for your stress hormones to hang out and percolate and govern your every move. You may notice less stress tolerance and more crankiness, sadness, irritation at others' mere presence, yelling at your partner, and other unwanted experiences. I like to call that "Fear Soup." You're sitting in a bunch of chemicals brought on by fear, which weakens you. In short, you're not preparing yourself for the worst; you're preparing yourself to not be able to handle the worst when it comes. You will have weakened yourself so much, you'll barely have enough energy to acknowledge that the shit has hit the fan. Even if your miracle were to actually happen, you'd be less likely to enjoy it. Further, just as quantum physics shows, when you attend to the shit hitting the fan, the Universe conspires to make that happen.

Yes, the difference between your miracle and the worst-case scenario is cavernous. Experiencing the worst-case scenario while holding on to the image of your miracle is extremely painful, and one might argue it's more painful than had you been "preparing" for the worst-case scenario all along. I hear you. Somehow we've been led to believe that by conjuring up worst-case scenarios in our minds, we're more capable of planning and handling them when they happen. If you're like me, this is the way you've been living for a long time. But it's an illusion.

It's important to note here again: Your fertility struggles are not your fault! You cannot change something you didn't realize was a problem. Love all the parts of yourself that have been re-creating your past and begin to do better. You've already started doing so throughout this book. Continue the journey with the following action steps.

Action Steps: Basking in Possibility

The following exercises are designed to help you wrap your mind around thinking in terms of possibility. These exercises are meant to be lighthearted and done in the spirit of fun. Your heart should feel lighter after having completed them. And after all that deep science just now, I know you can use a little lightness. I've got your back, love.

Exercise 1: Gratitude-ing

I once worked with a client who was telling me of her accomplishments since we'd last met, and she noted she had been doing her "gratitude-ing." I absolutely loved the implication of making gratitude an action, and I told her right then that I was stealing the word. The truth is, gratitude is a state of being, but it takes some work to get there. Our consciousness has all the intent, but it takes a while for our brains to catch up. This exercise is the practice of gratitude-ing, so you can reach the heretofore elusive state of gratitude.

Get your journal out for this one. Every day, twice a day, write three things you are grateful for. That's it.

AM: _____

_____

_____

PM: _____

_____

_____

It doesn't matter what those things are. I've written about loving the smell of oncoming rain or the fact that my slippers wait for me at the bottom of the stairs. Last night I delighted in how my dog smells. It's not always pleasant, mind you, but it means he's with me, and I love it. The point is, you'll be developing an awareness that things in your world right now are gorgeous, just right, and exactly as you'd like them to be. After a while, this will be second nature and you'll be more likely to notice the awesomeness that is your life rather than any crap that shows up. In addition, the crap will be easier to handle because of the awesomeness.

Exercise 2: The Remember-When Game

I was once at a training where I had the pleasure of meeting a gorgeous soul who introduced me to this game. Because I'm one who likes to pay gifts forward, I'm introducing it to you here. Some people find it very difficult to get into the headspace of their miracle happening. It's difficult when everything around you is evidence that you don't have your miracle yet. So, in the spirit of fun, I invite you to play the Remember-When Game. This is best played with your partner, but you can certainly play it just by writing your thoughts down in your journal.

Remembering when involves acting as if you're already in your future reality. Speak about today as if it were your past. Around your fertility struggles, the conversation with your partner might look like this:

Remember when we didn't have our baby yet? How anxious I was? How sad I was? Remember that time I wanted to pick up that one baby blanket because it had the cute monkeys on it and I felt so weird about it? Now our baby snuggles with it! Isn't that crazy? And remember when you had to give me those shots and how nervous you were? Looking back now, it's so hilarious. Oh! And remember when your sister was scared to tell us she was pregnant? Man, I felt so bad. Now I'm so grateful for her discretion, and she's, like, the best aunt ever!

If you're playing this game right, you'll both be reminiscing as if this is literally your past and everything is resolved now. Everything you've ever dreamed of has come to fruition. And just like our little man coming home from Korea, it will feel as if it always was. Have fun with this game! It's really a great time over a glass of wine; I know from personal experience.

Exercise 3: Noticing Synchronicities

I was once on a camping trip with my family, sitting by a riverbank and reading a book when I heard a hawk cawing. Pausing in my book, I watched as she seemingly floated above the river, hunting for a fish. She would dive into the water, make a big splash, emerge without a fish, and fly back to the east end of the river, slowly making her way back to where she'd previously noticed a fish. She dove in so many times that I lost count. After a good twenty minutes of this, I finally went back to my book. A few paragraphs later, my jaw dropped as I read the part of a scene where a bird repeatedly dove into a river in search of a fish. In my real life, the hawk was still fishing! I reread the paragraph and sat in total awe with a knowing smile on my face. That's a perfect example of synchronicity. How one interprets this is completely up to them. For me? I was struggling with a work issue, and the message I got from my intuition was to beef up my tenacity. I simply had to keep on keepin' on.

In this exercise, I'd like you to notice synchronicities that pop up for you as you experience gratitude and play the Remember-When Game. Instead of an infertility trigger, these synchronicities should elicit a sense of awe, wonder, and guidance. They should leave you like I was: in total awe with a knowing smile. Perhaps you'll even shake your head. Write down each time this happens, and watch the synchronicities pile up.

Fertility Mantra

Practice this mantra in the morning and in the evening for the next ten days.

Breathing in: All possibilities exist.

Breathing out: What I attend to becomes reality.

Breathing in: Miracles happen.

Breathing out: I can create miracles.

(Repeat three times.)

Fertility Meditation: The Bridge to the Other Side

Do this meditation daily for the next ten days. (Reminder: You can access my recordings of this and all other meditations from this book at www.drmariarothenburger.com/transcendingmeditations.)

Getting into a comfortable position, lying down or sitting up, back softly straight. Chin pointing slightly down. The crown of your head pulling slightly up from your neck and shoulders. Take three deep breaths…

Inhale…a loving light enters your body.

Exhale…negativity leaves.

Inhale…loving light.

Exhale…negativity leaves.

Inhale…

Exhale…

Imagine yourself now on a nature trail. Look around you. What do you see? It is superbly comfortable for you here; a place to simply be. What do you hear? Everything here is familiar, evokes a sense of wonder, and most of all you feel peaceful and calm here.

Continue moving on this trail. Up ahead you notice a slight change in the landscape. There's a bridge ahead. Walking to it, you get curious about what might be on the other side.

You've now reached the bridge. Standing at this end of the bridge, realizing that it's very safe and strong, take a look at what it's made of. What do you see? What is underneath the bridge? What do you see on the other side?

Moving across the bridge now and noticing all that nature has for you in this space. This bridge was created just for you. It is your own personal path to the other side of your struggles to have a baby.

You're now on the other side of the bridge. There is a path here as well, and it moves through some dense foliage to a clearing. This is the place where you meet your guides. Notice them. Perhaps it is only one guide, or perhaps it is many.

They have something to show you. Walking along the path with your guide now, you come upon a gorgeous scene. It's you on the other side of the struggle. This is the perfect resolution to your journey thus far. What do you see?

Who is here with you?

What feelings do you have as you see what's there on this side of the bridge?

Be with this scene for a little while…

Walking back to the clearing with your guide now, they remind you, this is the resolution to your story. It is on its way. You have more journeying to do, and the resolution is on its way. Look for it, feel it, know it. You are always guided and never alone.

Walking back to the bridge, feel a new sense of wonder, of delight, of comfort, knowing the other side of your journey is on its way.

Walk back over the bridge to your favorite safe spot, keeping the memory of what you just saw on the other side. Whenever you see a bridge or think of a bridge, remind yourself of your other side and feel the truth of it.

What's Next?

The next chapter is different. You've read the end of my fertility journey, culminating in a miraculous family of three. I've done much loving and living since then, and I intend to continue doing so. But first, attending to the beast that is infertility. I acknowledge its presence in my life, and I suspect it will never go away. I don't mind that. The next chapter is all about why I don't mind. I've written a letter to Infertility, and I invite you to read it now.

Chapter Ten

Dear Infertility

Out of suffering have emerged the strongest souls;
The most massive characters are seared with scars.
– Kahlil Gibran

Dear Infertility,

There's a story of an eight-foot-tall golden Buddha statue in Siam—now called Thailand—that was honored in a Buddhist monastery. The Buddhists there were fearful that the Burmese army was soon to invade the country, and they proceeded to cover the statue in clay in hopes that the army would simply pass the statue by. After all, there were thousands of Buddha statues all over the country. There was no reason to suspect the invaders would be interested in a run-of-the-mill clay statue. The monks were right. The Burmese army invaded Siam, and happening upon the Buddha statue, now clad in a cloak of gray clay, they ignored it and moved on to other pillaging.

Hundreds of years later, in 1957, the Buddha statue was being moved to a new location. The machine that was lifting it was straining under the weight of the statue, much to the perplexity of the monks. At some point, the machine operator let the statue down, and the monks intended to finish the relocation project later the next day. That evening it began to rain. A monk went out to the statue in an attempt to cover it and noticed that there was a crack in the statue, likely from when it was placed in its current spot. As the monk looked closer, however, he noticed something shiny deep down in the crevice of the crack. He invited other monks to help chip away more of the clay covering, and soon the entire solid gold Buddha statue was in full view of mystified monks. The statue now sits in its Thai home, to be honored forever.

Dearest Infertility, this Buddha statue metaphor is what I am grateful to you for. My fellow fertility-seeking family and I were born golden. But then we grew up. We lived in our families, went to school, and were given labels and told what we were "supposed" to do with our lives. We were told we must meet someone, get married, buy a house, have 2.5 children and a yellow lab, etc. Eventually, we unlearned the truth of our golden spirit and became clad in gray concrete. Like the clay Buddha statue, we considered ourselves in the image of, but certainly not, the Divine.

Then, Infertility, you came into my life and cracked the concrete casing with your penetrating, traumatic blow. Inch by aching inch, more of the concrete was painfully chipped away until my raw, open soul was displayed for the world to see. Most importantly, it was displayed for me to see. Broken open, I saw myself for who I truly am. The golden hues are a mystery, even though they've always been a part of me. I see myself in the Divine and the Divine in me. Now, because of you, I know who I am. I am part of the Divine. I am beauty. I am peace. I am fertile. Because of you, the armor and concrete will never satisfy me again. I know the truth. I'm like a piece of Japanese kintsugi pottery—my cracks are accentuated with gold.

Some people say this is crazy. How could anyone possibly be grateful for infertility? Let's be honest, Infertility. You're an asshole. You make life unbearable. You increase worry, anxiety, sadness, and nightmares. You make people lose friends and have suicidal thoughts, and you ruin marriages. You make people wonder how they could ever endure such fear and devastation. People lose themselves in darkness, anxiety, and "less than" thinking. I recall the vivid thoughts of things like "I must not be good enough to be a mom." "I must have done something really bad to deserve this." "I suck." "The Universe must think I'd be a terrible mom. It's probably right." How could it ever be okay to create this despair? You rip hearts out and leave tender souls vulnerably exposed to the elements. Why?

I now know why.

Because sometimes creating profound beauty requires first being broken. I had to be broken before I could allow the light to shine in. Even to myself. I had to feel myself in all my brokenness in order to know who I really am. I came to know that, in my broken, imperfect, marred spirit, I was still very much whole. I was a piece of the Universe, of God, of Spirit, or Source—whatever one calls the Love energy that permeates everything. I am That. You are That.

I am so grateful to you, Infertility. I would not know of my internal beauty without you. Flailing around in, then emerging from the trauma, I noticed a few things that have changed for the better because of you. The following are the five aspects of Posttraumatic Growth and how I changed in each:

Personal Strength

- I do not expect myself to be perfect.
- I laugh at myself and my mistakes.
- I respect, honor, and am compassionate toward myself when I mess up.
- I am flexible, allowing for shitstorms to come my way, and I don't collapse in the process.
- I feel my feelings without *being* my feelings.

New Possibilities

- I am excited for what's next in life, even if the next thing is hard.
- I don't need to control anything.
- I am openly and lovingly curious about possibilities.
- The kid in me has emerged; I play with everything just to see what will happen. It's fun!
- I still screw up (a lot!), and I wait to see how that will move me toward growth.

Relating to Others

- I do not expect T to be different than who he is.
- I will never, ever pressure or ask anyone about when they'll have a baby.
- I will never pressure or ask anyone about any part of their future existence; I am excited for who they are right now.
- I want to give, give, give to others. (Interestingly, this results in me receiving.)
- I see people for their humanness, not their faults and follies.

Appreciation of Life

- I look at parenthood as an unbelievable blessing *and* can appreciate that it's also friggin' hard.
- I notice sparkles of sunshine on water, trees rustling in the wind, and the sounds of birds singing their tune in a given moment.
- I am okay with what is, rather than needing things to be different from what they are.
- I feel abundant, secure, and believe that all good things are coming my way (even if it means some crap shows up, too).
- I am deeply grateful for every little thing I have right now in this singular moment.
- Even before our baby came, I had an appreciation for all we had. I no longer felt the gaping hole of non-parenthood. I felt complete.

Spiritual Change

- I believe that things are on their way to me, even when what I can see, hear, and feel is precisely the opposite.
- I feel guided. There is a presence beyond my tangible self that lovingly directs me. It doesn't matter what that energy is called—God, Universe, Creator, Great Spirit, my Greater Self—I now feel its loving presence moment to moment.

- All my experiences are meaningful. And I can affect what experiences I will have.
- I feel whole.
- I feel like myself.
- I love myself.

As I see it, Infertility, the pattern I've experienced with you has been one of total disbelief, then fear, then anger, then acceptance, and finally, gratitude. When I first met you, you were like an unwelcome stranger that tracked mud all over my newly mopped floors. I was mildly annoyed by you. I also thought cleaning your mess would take little more than a bit of soap, water, and elbow grease. Everything else in my life had been that way, and I knew that you were no different. Just do what the doctors say, Maria. Everything will fall into place, and you'll soon have your little munchkin in your arms.

You proved to be a much stronger adversary than even the doctors anticipated. You proved to be an adversary that took away all semblance of my ability to govern myself, to intuitively know what I needed, and to move forward with what I knew to be right for me. When I realized I couldn't control you, a rush of anxiety became my new constant companion. As the pages of this book illustrate, I was afraid of many particulars of life. Pregnancy announcements and baby showers are obvious, but the quiet yet insidious events and nuances were what I feared the most. When T and I would hang out with friends who had no children, I couldn't stay in the present moment for fear there would be a pregnancy announcement or someone would ask me when we were planning on having kids. I feared that an assumption would be made that I was pregnant, because I wasn't drinking alcohol. Combined with my IVF bloat, the assumption would not be that far-fetched. I intensely feared being called out for being pregnant when in fact my soul was dying to be a mom, and my body was not cooperating. Life began feeling like one big ball of fear.

Then came the anger, Infertility. You're amazing at bringing that out in people. And I got really great at utilizing sarcasm and biting, hurtful language to assuage my own internal fire while simultaneously hurting other people. The anger was all-consuming, kept me awake at night, prevented me from smiling casually at even the cutest of baby's smiles. I was pissed. And I felt you mocking me with every single negative pregnancy test and progesterone-in-oil shot T had to stick in my hindquarters. I was angry at the buckets of needles and chemicals I had to put into my body. I was angry at the bruises, the prick marks, the inability to sit well due to pain from shots, the regular internal sonograms that invaded my privacy every other (extremely early) morning, the irony of looking several months pregnant, the bags under my eyes, the hair loss, the friend loss, the memory loss, the love loss, the happiness loss, the life loss. I was angry that I wasn't myself anymore. I was angry that I could no longer be that innocent soul riding the wave of life, like, "Yup, I've so got this." You knocked me off my wave and into the depths of the sea where I got snagged on a piece of garbage and had to fight for the life I knew was floating above me. I could see it through the murky, undulating water—blue skies, birds, joy—but I couldn't get free from the garbage holding me just under the surface.

I struggled for what seemed an eternity in that angry space. Covered by the murky depths of sea, I didn't know that the more I struggled, the more I got stuck. I would not let go of the anger because I thought it was the one thing I could control. I was wrong. As terrifying as it was, I realized that what I was doing with my life didn't move me toward my goal even half an iota. Because of this, I decided to let go. In rushed the fear of letting go, like a towering wave that threatened to drown me. And I let go anyway. I felt all the fear and let go anyway.

It was at this point that acceptance began making its way into the depths of my muted existence and slowly pulled me up into the salty air and sunshine. Not being completely steady on my feet, I didn't trust acceptance at first, yet it showed up for me no matter how many times I asked for it. With a tranquility I hadn't known for many years, acceptance swaddled me and gave me a cup of hot tea to warm my broken spirits. Achingly slowly, I began to pick up the pieces of my broken-pottery self and began the mending process. This is when the beauty of everything I'd been through became obvious to me. I was a new human. I had scars to show my humanness, but I was still too shy, meek, and timid to show them or to find peace in them. After a while, I began to polish the pieces of myself and put them back together. And they were beautiful.

Realizing my messy, broken, fissure-riddled self was beautiful, I moved right into gratitude for you, Infertility. For so long, you'd been the insidious, painful, and then dominating, negative force in my life. I didn't know you were actually like an annoying fitness coach who causes me pain, insists I can go further and longer, lift more weight, move faster—the one I curse every time I head to the gym and yet the one I owe a debt of gratitude to for my newfound svelte body. However, the strength you've given me in mind and spirit has far surpassed anything the sweaty fitness coach could have instilled in me. You helped me create a better version of myself than I ever thought possible. I love you for moving me toward loving myself. In the words of that beautiful song by Alanis Morrissette, "Thank you, terror. Thank you, disillusionment. Thank you, frailty…" Thank you, Infertility. Thank you.

Love always,
Maria

Fertility Key: No Mud, No Lotus

The book *No Mud, No Lotus: The Art of Transforming Suffering*, written by the beautiful Buddhist monk Thich Nhat Hanh, is a lovely guide to making our suffering useful. It describes how the lotus flower grows out of mud and therefore cannot exist without the mud. Some people say the lotus fights and strains its way out of the mud, but I disagree. I say it lies in wait, soaking up the rich nutrients in the mud until it is ready to slowly and gently emerge, a healthier, more gorgeous version of itself. It doesn't judge the mud. It simply blooms where it's planted.

You have ultimate control over your reaction to painful things. Most humans want to run away from pain, right? We have an incessant need to feel calm and peaceful, yet running from pain is not the way to calm and peace. In a book by the comedian Kyle Cease, *I Hope I Screw This Up*, he writes, "Allowing yourself to fully experience every emotion that you feel is the gateway to transformation." It's incredibly important to feel all your feelings because that's where the good stuff is. Instead of lamenting them, you have an opportunity to use your painful feelings for nourishment and growth. Just as the lotus flower emerges from the mud, see painful emotions as encouragement that you are growing as a human. No need to force the growth. Allow it to happen. Eventually you will experience wisdom from your pain.

> It's incredibly important to feel all your feelings because that's where the good stuff is. Instead of lamenting them, you have an opportunity to use your painful feelings for nourishment and growth.

As Dr. Joe Dispenza says, "The memory without the intense emotional reaction is called wisdom." Wisdom is in your future because you'll be using your painful emotional experience as your greatest teacher. Feel the fear of this and do it anyway.

The action steps below are designed to help you notice both the crap and the good stuff that have come out of your fertility struggles. If you can't seem to find good stuff, just stick with neutral for now. You're an emerging lotus flower, after all. Patience is important.

About Posttraumatic Stress

I'd be remiss if I didn't mention here that posttraumatic growth and posttraumatic stress are not mutually exclusive. That is, you can experience both at the same time. You can be a gorgeous lotus flower still in the mud! Posttraumatic stress is a heightened awareness and body response to a stressful, traumatic event. I still occasionally have stressful responses to pregnant bellies, pregnancy announcements, baby showers, and the like. The difference is, I welcome them as opportunities for continued growth. I hug that part of myself that's still in pain.

If, however, you have significant symptoms of posttraumatic stress, it may serve you well to seek a professional to help you move through the difficulty. It is a beautiful thing to lean on someone else as a guide for a while.

Action Steps: Growing a Lotus out of the Mud

Exercise 1: Adding Up the Goods

I once met with a client who told me of her ability to see the good that came out of infertility. In her home, she had a jar of jelly beans. Sticking up out of the jelly beans were skewers with notes about her blessings. "Whenever I have a hard day, I add a jelly bean, and when I notice my blessings, I add another note." Before long, she was able to see there was more good than crap. Isn't that cool? For this exercise, I'd love for you to do something similar. You can make your own jelly bean/skewer jar, or you can create your own thing.

There's only one difference I would highlight here, and that is to intentionally connect your blessings or good things to the crap. This helps you create meaning from having to experience a hard thing. What is one neutral or good thing that came out of the hard thing? If you're keeping track in your journal, it might look like this:

Mud of the Day:

_____

Lotus that Came from the Mud:

_____

The point is to notice that some things are better because of having to experience the crap. Not all things, mind you, but a healthy percentage of the crap brings you good stuff.

Someone else I worked with recently noted that she felt unproductive during times of sadness; her mud of the day would be experiencing sadness. Her lotus would be the ability to slow down and take care of herself (rather than having to be ultra productive). In the beginning, you'll likely have to hunt for the good (or the neutral); after a while, it becomes obvious.

Note: Noticing the good does not mean negating your pain! I'm not asking you to wear rose-colored glasses and ignore the crap. I'm asking you to honor both with your loving attention.

Exercise 2: Write a Letter to Infertility

How could I not highlight this exercise for you? I suggest writing this as a journal entry when you have a lot of time and privacy. You may get this all out on paper however you wish. Maybe it'll be a series of disconnected words about infertility. Maybe it'll be drawings or other types of artwork. Maybe you'll write a paragraph and come back to finish it later. Maybe it'll be a long, ongoing letter that you write throughout your whole journey. The only thing that matters is that you tell Infertility what you want it to know.

This letter does not need to be like mine. You don't need to see yet how Infertility has helped you. That will hopefully come in time. What's most important is that you acknowledge the infertility experience in your life and tell it what you think it should know. It's been bossing you around for a while, right? This is your turn to boss it around (always with love, of course).

Fertility Mantra

Practice this mantra in the morning and in the evening for the next ten days.

Breathing in: Feelings are intense.

Breathing out: I feel them anyway.

Breathing in: Infertility is intense.

Breathing out: I have grown because of it.

(Repeat three times.)

Fertility Meditation: Radical Self-Compassion

Do this meditation daily for the next ten days. (Reminder: You can access my recordings of this and all other meditations from this book at www.drmariarothenburger.com/transcendingmeditations.)

This guided meditation is designed to help you begin to develop compassion toward yourself. Guided imagery is used here to elicit an emotional response. However, the images are not as important as the feelings.

Don't worry if you cannot envision what is said in this meditation. Simply notice any feelings that come up and pay the most attention to those that feel good.

Let's begin by helping relax your mind and body through a body scan. Imagine a light above you, about the size of marble. It's a soft pulsating light in whatever color is most relaxing and meaningful for you. It might be white. Or a soft turquoise, pink, or orange. Perhaps it's a combination of colors. It only matters that it feels good to you.

You see this little light becoming larger and larger. It pulsates out while hovering above your body and begins to slowly descend over you. What temperature does this light have? What sensations does it produce in your body? Tingling? Cooling? Warmth? Or a vibration?

The light has fully enveloped you now. It's like a comforting hug. You are completely safe and protected here.

Now, notice how the light makes your feet feel. Notice any tension there and watch it melt away. If any thoughts come into your mind that are not related to the light and your feet—and they will—it's completely okay. Just noticing that your mind wandered and bringing it back to the light.

How's the light feeling in your legs? Is there tension there? Noticing now the muscles in your legs beginning to be completely soft. All of your leg muscles completely relaxed.

And now your belly. There might be a lot of tension here you never noticed. Or if you've gotten skilled at fully relaxing, you might notice a relative lack of tension. See if you can relax even more. Ah, the light soothes your stomach and all of the organs within. They gently do their job with no tension at all.

And now, feel how your upper torso and arms are enveloped in your soft glowing and pulsing light. Notice how your shoulders have dropped away from your ears. The light holds them up without any effort from you. The light supports you. There is nothing you need to do.

You now notice your face. Letting go of any stress and tension, noticing your brow completely placid and even the muscles behind your eyes have let go. You are so supported and relaxed now. And you either feel so weightless you are floating, or you feel immensely grounded into the earth. Either way, you are totally supported.

Now, imagine you are in a particularly familiar and comfortable place in your home. As you imagine this place, what are you enjoying there? Notice everything. Is it daytime? What are the noises around you? Who's there with you? What does it smell like? What are you sitting or lying on? Just be here for a moment.

Your comfort is suddenly disrupted by a phone call. The caller ID says the name of someone very important to you and you take the call immediately. This person is in distress. Something terrible has happened, and they hardly have the breath to explain. You take a deep breath enough for the both of you.

Inhale…

And exhale…

As they're speaking to you, you move around in your home getting ready to go to them. They explain they've made a terrible mistake, and they express deep shame and fear. Notice your feelings as you listen to their voice. What is your impulse? How do you feel about the potential of comforting them?

You make your way to them in any way your imagination takes you—by foot, bicycle, or car—and eventually you come upon their home. You alert them you're there, and you wait for them to open the door. Notice your feelings as you wait. Suddenly you hear the doorknob moving and the squeak of the opening door. You see the light from inside the home, and experience a shock of recognition as you see who has invited you in.

It's you. You see the anguish on your own face. You know that your heart is breaking. You know you've experienced a great loss. What do you want to tell this person who is so close to you? What do you want to offer them? They are, after all, you. Perhaps in the past you've wanted to scold yourself, to tell yourself you're wrong or bad in some way. Now, see yourself as you would a very close friend.

What would you like to say instead? You invite yourself in. See yourself taking care of you, hugging you, offering words of comfort. Offering worldly support like tea or comfort foods. Mostly, though, you see in your own eyes compassionate understanding. You see gentleness, you see kindness, you see love. You see yourself saying not just, "I feel for you," you're saying, "I feel *with* you."

Perhaps you have nothing brilliant to say to make the pain disappear, but you do have your presence. And that can be healing enough.

Take a moment now, to come back to the room you are in. Take a deep breath in. And exhale. Noticing the sensations in the room, noticing what you're sitting or lying on, notice the sounds around you. Wiggle your toes and fingers to alert yourself you are back in the present moment. In your own space. Remember to own all of who you are. Your hits and misses. Your wins and your mistakes. Your losses. And your gains.

And use those experiences as guidance for your future rather than reasons to be harmful to yourself. Just like your closest friend, you deserve respect, honor, and most of all, compassion. And so it is.

Conclusion

The Beginning

Thank you terror
Thank you providence
Thank you disillusionment
Thank you nothingness
Thank you clarity
Thank you, thank you silence
– Alanis Morrissette

This is the beginning of a new you. Do not take that sentence lightly. After having completed the exercises in this book, you will have gently begun a new way of looking at not only your fertility journey but all of life. The reason this book's title contains an "ing" word—*transcending*—is because the journey never stops. I hope you continue to use the skills from this book for your continued growth throughout your life, always moving toward conceiving new things (fertility isn't just for making babies, after all), creating miracles, and improving on your humanity. These skills are meant to help you change yourself and watch the ripple effect unfold. You won't be able to stop it. You'll get to see others improve simply because they get to be in your life. Isn't that an awesome responsibility? It all starts with you. Right now.

In the years since our parenthood journey, T and I have moved cross country, gotten new jobs, settled in new homes, and added to our family (both fur and human babies). All these experiences have been wrapped in uncertainty, stress, and lack of control. Friggin' life, right? It's only due to the lessons described in this book that I've been able to move through these things fluidly, with greater ease, and with more grace than I'd previously had.

Have there been infertility triggers? Holy shit—yes. When we adopted our second son, for example, I was stuck in Chicago for what seemed an eternity while waiting for paperwork to move through the legal system. Everything was out of my control. I sobbed, I lost sleep, I panicked. The second I realized I was experiencing an infertility trigger, I was able to honor it without needing it to go away. I simply allowed the panic to wash over me, and it likely settled far sooner than it would have had I attempted to ignore it. And it certainly would have stuck around longer had I chastised myself for being "weak." You too will experience triggers; I can promise you that. But this is the beginning of a new you, remember? You are more powerful, more graceful, more capable of producing miracles than you've ever thought. By working on this book's exercises, you've been working toward getting yourself back.

I've worked with people who wish to be themselves again. I will not mince words when I tell you that you will never be like you used to be. That version of you is gone due to the trauma of infertility. It's important to honor who you used to be, the parts of you that you miss, and the parts of you that you may never see again. On the other side of that honor, however, is the recognition that you're a better version of yourself because of everything you've been through. Look at the parts of yourself that were perhaps less than stellar. How are you changed now? Or how about those things that were already pretty good? How much better are they? After completing this book's exercises, you may notice a greater awareness of your strength. You may notice a gentleness toward yourself that was not there previously. Maybe you're less perfectionistic. Maybe you're able to notice all the parts of your life that are not infertility related. You're an amazing human, and you're even more amazing after having experienced infertility. I'm not overstating things here. By virtue of riding the roller coaster of infertility and continuing to breathe, you are amazing.

If you take nothing else from the pages of this book and from your own experience in completing these exercises, let it be this: All the answers are within. You never again need to seek outside yourself for answers to your questions. If you have a problem with something external to yourself, look inside and see how something inside you can be adjusted to have a healthier reaction. Do you still hold tight to anger? Do you should on yourself and other people? Are you ignoring your intuition? There is nothing bad about these experiences. In the therapy world, we like to say it's all grist for the therapeutic mill. Use any negativity as another clue toward being a better human. You're well on your way already. Congratulations.

Paying it Forward

The program outlined in this book is largely focused on how you treat yourself. What's interesting about this is that once you become kinder, more compassionate, and more loving toward yourself, you begin to treat others this way too. That's why I wrote this book: to be of service to others. That has become my reason for existing; it makes me feel whole inside. I have so much to give. And I can't seem to stop giving. Can you imagine a life like that? What would it look like?

Have you ever seen the movie (or read the book) *Pay It Forward*? It's based on the idea that if you're kind to one person, that person will be kind to at least one other person (oftentimes, many more), and then those people are kind to at least one person, and so on. In this way, kindness can spread like wildfire. And it all starts with how you treat yourself. Once you treat yourself kindly, you'll have an abundance of kindness to pay forward to many others who will pay it forward to others, ad infinitum.

So, to take the program in this book one step further: seek opportunities to be kind to yourself so that you can pay it forward to others. The world could do with a little bit (or a lot) of kindness. And however your fertility journey is finally resolved, living in a kinder world is a fantastic goal, with or without kids.

A Picture of the New You

You are a person of great integrity. You know when you need to set limits with others because you're in pain from an infertility trigger. You wear your infertility masks only when absolutely needed, and you take them off to take care of yourself most of the time. You allow the pain of infertility triggers to wash over you, and they go away faster. Because you allow the pain to exist without running away from it, the joy in your life becomes more prominent than in the past. You're able to do things that bring a smile to your face. You experience belly laughs and get caught up in fun moments with your partner, friends, and family.

You now notice when you need to fill your own cup with self-care, which you consider an essential part of life. You know that in order to truly be helpful to others, you must first be helpful to yourself. You know now that when you notice that someone else's behavior is upsetting to you, you need to notice what it is about yourself that needs kindness and compassion in order to tolerate better. You make growing your family very important, but it is no longer a desperate longing. It is something you know is on its way. You trust.

Because you are now gifted at moving through hard times with ease, you recover relatively quickly from difficult news. You know exactly what support you need, and you ask others to assist whenever you need extra love. You no longer feel ashamed. You no longer feel chronically angry. You no longer hold on to the supposed control that has actually held you back. You know that miracles are on their way to you, even if everything in the material world points directly to the opposite.

Intimacy with your partner explodes. They understand exactly what you need in moments of distress because you're able to tell them clearly. You are also able to support them and receive any feedback they give with ease.

You're able to communicate effectively with relatives, friends, and others who don't know exactly what you're going through. There's a lack of bitterness now, as you explain what you need from them. There's a lack of anger when they still don't understand; you are gentle and easy. And when you're not in touch with your own gentleness and ease, you recognize the need to retreat and take care of yourself.

You're able to sit in stillness. You don't need to stay busy to be away from your thoughts. Stillness is a welcome experience because you feel peaceful inside now. Gone are the chronic desperation, the bitterness, the anger, the pain. But if those things do show up, you honor them, and they become quiet again.

Everyone feels your peace. They want to be around you. You willingly give them some of your peace, knowing you can take care of yourself and refill your peace anytime you'd like. And by virtue of living a more peaceful life, your body responds in kind, kicking on your parasympathetic nervous system, healing cells, and improving your creative capacity (fertility and other creative endeavors).

You are open to possibility. You look forward to miracles. You create miracles. Watch them happen. This is only the beginning.

All these things—and more—are my wishes for you. And most of my wishes come true—just sayin'. May you also know within the depths of your being that your wishes—your miracles—are on their way to you.

And so it is.

Acknowledgments

For my fellow IFers: You're the reason.

To my former and current clients: You inspire me in ways you may not know. Thank you for entrusting your journey to me.

To my beta readers: You took the time and energy to read through the raw version of this manuscript, a task that even I didn't want to undertake! Your insights were invaluable, and I thank you from the bottom of my heart for your time and willingness to help me be more clear and to offer more value to future readers.

To Jodi Chapman, Dan Teck, and the Your Soulful Book (YSB) community: I wanted gentle prodding to get this manuscript complete, and you delivered just that. With your ongoing encouragement, dedication to success, and overdelivering value, this book finally made it out into the world! Plus you're just beautiful humans. I am beyond grateful to you.

To my editor who wishes to remain anonymous: It has never felt so good to be corrected. I giggled every time you mentioned "splitting hairs," and I laughed out loud (in tandem with a loving eye roll) when you gave me a literary lesson just for the seeming fun of it. I am beyond grateful to you and your belief in this project enough to take it on, even though you don't technically edit anymore. I shall continue working on single spacing after periods (still tripping out about that!), but I have to admit it's going to be a long while (dang habits).

To C and K: Thank you for being among my biggest cheerleaders. Thank you for FaceTime chats with wine (and sometimes whine) to commiserate about all things life pre- and post-fertility journey. And thanks for allowing me to share part of your precious journeys in this book.

To Diane Browne: Seriously, how do you see through all my infertility masks? You were there when we began trying to conceive and through all the magic since then. Thank you for not running away screaming when I was my raw, vulnerable self. And for letting me play in your sand tray.

To Mom and Lane: I am beyond grateful for your presence in our lives. Before human kids came along, you acknowledged our parenthood to our furbabies, and that will stay with me forever. It's incredibly delightful to hear our boys call you Grandma and Papa; thank you for sharing so much of your lives with them and us. I love you.

To D: I'd sing you some wind-beneath-my-wings cheesy song, but I'll save it for when we have another movie marathon and a few too many drinks (if that's a thing). You're the little sister that every other little sister has to live up to. Thank you so much for your candid feedback, for believing in me, for being okay with allowing me to share part of your story in this book, and for letting me be my quirky, nerdy self. You're almost too cool to be my sister. Almost. Love you beyond words.

To T: You and me, babe. You and me.

To O: You were (and are!) so wanted, my beautiful boy. When you read this someday, I hope that message from your coming-home story is loud and clear. Thank you for being your wild, prankster self during this whole project. You are good for the soul, and I love being your mom (but no more plastic wrap on the toilet seat, okay?). To B: My beloved youngest, it's been absolutely magical seeing you blossom into the musical, super silly, air-guitar loving little guy that you are. I look forward to many more dances around the house with you while blasting music.

To Bailey, Dexter, and Jake: You are my first kids. Thank you for training me well to be a good (imperfect) mama and for teaching me that it's really fun to delight in even the tiniest things life brings our way.

About the Author

Maria T. Rothenburger, PhD, LPC, CHt, is a professional counselor and coach specializing in family-building issues. She has spent the last ten years supporting people experiencing the devastating emotional, physical, and spiritual impact of fertility struggles. You can discover more about Maria and her work at www.drmariarothenburger.com and listen to her unique perspectives as host of the Miracles Happen Fertility Podcast. Maria enjoys learning piano and ukulele, singing, wine tasting, laughing daily, and living life in Oregon with her husband and five kids (two humans, two canines, and one feline).

Made in the USA
Columbia, SC
07 May 2021